"Lawrence Venuti is short-t[...] there's too much of both be[...] translation is (under)valued. The truth is that there is no truth, only interpretation. Venuti tangles with high-wire philosophers of language but wins his points mixing it up with film subtitlers on the rugged terrain of practical examples. Freed from self-constraint, translation can get on with critical, indeed radical, cultural work."
—DUDLEY ANDREW, R. Selden Rose Professor of Comparative Literature and Professor of Film Studies at Yale University

"Lawrence Venuti can always be relied upon to challenge facile assumptions about translation. In this exciting new book he explains how translation is always an act of interpretation and therefore there can be no such thing as an untranslatable. Anyone interested in understanding translation should read this account."
—SUSAN BASSNETT, professor emerita of comparative literature at the University of Warwick

"Every text is translatable because every text can be interpreted: with this provocation Lawrence Venuti challenges us to overhaul our thinking about translation by jettisoning the instrumentalist bias that has, according to him, plagued translation since Western antiquity. Instead, he proposes that we pursue translation as hermeneutics, episteme, discourse, and artifact; he asks that we treat receiving contexts with the kind of finesse we tend to reserve for source materials and restore to translation its overdue status as full-fledged conceptual labor in its own right. Written with a literary comparatist's erudite command of his field, *Contra Instrumentalism* is an exemplary critical statement on a transnational topic."
—REY CHOW, Anne Firor Scott Professor of Literature at Duke University

Contra Instrumentalism

SERIES EDITORS · *Marco Abel and Roland Végső*

PROV
OCAT
IONS

Something in the world forces us to think.
—Gilles Deleuze

The world provokes thought. Thinking is nothing but the human response to this provocation. Thus, the very nature of thought is to be the product of a provocation. This is why a genuine act of provocation cannot be the empty rhetorical gesture of the contrarian. It must be an experimental response to the historical necessity to act. Unlike the contrarian, we refuse to reduce provocation to a passive noun or a state of being. We believe that real moments of provocation are constituted by a series of actions that are best defined by verbs or even infinitives— verbs in a modality of potentiality, of the promise of action. To provoke is to intervene in the present by invoking an as yet undecided future radically different from what is declared to be possible in the present and, in so doing, to arouse the desire for bringing about change. By publishing short books from multiple disciplinary perspectives that are closer to the genres of the manifesto, the polemical essay, the intervention, and the pamphlet than to traditional scholarly monographs, "Provocations" hopes to serve as a forum for the kind of theoretical experimentation that we consider to be the very essence of thought.

www.provocationsbooks.com

Contra Instrumentalism

A Translation Polemic

LAWRENCE VENUTI

UNIVERSITY OF NEBRASKA PRESS · LINCOLN

Grateful acknowledgment is made to
Duke University Press for permission to
republish material that first appeared in
"Hijacking Translation: How Comp Lit
Continues to Suppress Translated Texts,"
boundary 2 43, no. 1 (2016): 179–204.

Library of Congress
Cataloging-in-Publication Data

Names: Venuti, Lawrence, author.
Title: Contra instrumentalism: a
translation polemic / Lawrence Venuti.
Description: Lincoln: University of
Nebraska Press, 2019. | Series: Provocations
| Includes bibliographical references.
Identifiers: LCCN 2018047747
ISBN 9781496205131 (paperback: alk. paper)
ISBN 9781496215925 (epub)
ISBN 9781496215932 (mobi)
ISBN 9781496215949 (pdf)
Subjects: LCSH: Translating and interpreting—
Philosophy. | Instrumentalism (Philosophy)
Classification: LCC P306 .V36
2019 | DDC 418/.02—dc23
LC record available at
https://lccn.loc.gov/2018047747

Set in Sorts Mill Goudy by E. Cuddy.
Designed by N. Putens.

CONTENTS

ACKNOWLEDGMENTS

My work on this book received helpful comments from colleagues, some of whom read portions at various stages of completion: Rey Chow, Michael Cronin, Brent Hayes Edwards, Trevor Margraf, Dan O'Hara, Marjorie Perloff, Nirvana Tanoukhi, and Susan Wells. Gary Gutting made some useful remarks about Michel Foucault's work. Roger Celestin, Augusto Lorenzino, Steven Rendall, and Chantal Wright provided information that aided with the introduction.

The first chapter began as a response on the panel, "Debating World Literature," at the Institute for World Literature held at Harvard University on June 28, 2013. I would like to thank the director, David Damrosch, for the opportunity to speak there. Sally Mitchell led me to useful data on Victorian housing. Susan Bernofsky described the activities of the Occupy Wall Street Translation Working Group. Matthew Harrington shared his research into the Spanish impact of Stéphane Hessel's *Indignez-vous!* An earlier version of the chapter appeared in the journal *boundary 2*. I thank the editor, Paul Bové, and the editorial collective for their support.

With Marie-Alice Belle in Linguistics and Translation at the University of Montreal I had enlightening exchanges on early modern translation. Gina Psaki in Romance Languages at the University of Oregon directed me to essential research on the proverb, "traduttore traditore." Paolo Cherchi, emeritus in Italian and Spanish at the University of Chicago, kindly vetted my translation of an excerpt from Niccolò Franco's text. Paul Howard in Italian at Trinity College, Cambridge, helped me fine-tune my choices for that translation.

Lucien Brown in Korean linguistics at the University of Oregon patiently answered my questions about the Korean language and provided transliterations of Hangul characters. I received assistance with the soundtrack of Park Chan-wook's film *Thirst* from Da Ye Kim, who provided transcriptions and transliterations and replied to my queries about specific words and phrases. I am grateful for the illuminating interviews given by a number of subtitlers, including Henri Béhar, Lenny Borger, John Guldej, Wonjo Jeong, and Esther Kwon. Peter Becker and Liz Helfgott provided information about the Criterion Collection. Peter Connor in French and Comparative Literature at Barnard College transcribed the soundtrack for the opening scenes of Jules Dassin's *Rififi* with the assistance of Elsa Connor.

All unattributed translations and transcriptions are mine.

Karen Van Dyck felt it all, inevitably, and responded with encouragement, criticism, arguments pro and con, and the loveliest atmosphere(s) in which to live and work.

L.V.
New York–Barcelona–Syros
June 2018

PROVOCATIONS

Translation is and always has been ubiquitous. Today it figures significantly in the practices housed in many cultural and social institutions—economic and political, legal and military, religious and scientific. The arts and human sciences depend on translation for their invention, accumulation, and dissemination of forms and ideas. Nonetheless, translation remains grossly misunderstood, ruthlessly exploited, and blindly stigmatized. Now is the time to abandon the simplistic, clichéd thinking that has limited our understanding of it for millennia.

STOP treating translation as a metaphor.
START considering it a material practice that is indivisibly linguistic *and* cultural.

STOP using moralistic terms like "faithful" and "unfaithful" to describe translation.
START defining it as the establishment of a variable equivalence to the source text.

STOP assuming that translation is mechanical substitution.
START conceiving of it as an interpretation that demands writerly and intellectual sophistication.

STOP evaluating translations merely by comparing them to the source text.

START examining their relations to the hierarchy of values, beliefs, and representations in the receiving culture.

STOP asserting that any text is untranslatable.

START realizing that every text is translatable because every text can be interpreted.

Contra Instrumentalism

START/STOP

Scope

The target of this polemic is a model of translation that I shall call *instrumentalism*. It conceives of translation as the reproduction or transfer of an invariant that is contained in or caused by the source text, an invariant form, meaning, or effect. Not only has this model dominated translation theory and commentary for more than two millennia, but its continued dominance can be seen in both elite and popular cultures, in academic institutions and in publishing, in scholarly monographs and in literary journalism, in the most rarefied theoretical discourses and in the most commonly used clichés and proverbs about translation. The negative consequences of this dominance have included the inferior ranking of translation practice in the hierarchy of scholarly and literary rewards, the relative paucity, reductiveness, and sheer naïveté of translation research, and a set of theoretical concepts and practical strategies that preempt a rather different model of translation that I shall call *hermeneutic*.

A hermeneutic model conceives of translation as an interpretive act that inevitably varies source-text form, meaning, and effect according to intelligibilities and interests in the receiving culture. The variation occurs even when the translator, like most translators today, adheres to a fairly strict concept of equivalence that seeks to construct both a semantic correspondence and a stylistic approximation to the source text. According to the hermeneutic model I will advance here, adapted in part from the semiotic theory of Charles Peirce and Umberto Eco,[1] a translator turns a source text into a translation by applying *interpretants*, factors that are formal (such as a concept of equivalence or a concept of style) and thematic (such as an interpretation of the source text presented elsewhere in commentary or an ideology in the sense of an ensemble of values, beliefs, and representations affiliated with particular social groups). The interpretants, often applied intuitively and without critical reflection, not only guide the translator's verbal choices but ensure that they are more than merely verbal, that they effectively constitute interpretive moves which inform and nuance various textual structures and meanings, including prosody and imagery, narrative point of view and characterization, genre and discourse, terminology and argument. The application of interpretants guarantees that a translation is relatively autonomous from its source text even while establishing a variety of interpretive relations to that text.

Although the interpretants may contain source-cultural materials, they are drawn predominantly from the receiving culture where the decision to translate is often made, especially with texts in humanistic fields and disciplines like literature and philosophy. Nonetheless, a translation does not simply assimilate the source text to what is intelligible and interesting to receptors. By maintaining a semantic correspondence and stylistic approximation, a translation can provide a basis for various accounts of the source text, including plot summaries and character analyses, summaries of philosophical arguments and explications of conceptual terms, descriptions of lexical and syntactical features as well as their coalescence into a distinctive style. Still, none of the interpretive relations established by the translation can be understood as giving back the source text unaltered or as enabling a reader to respond to the translation in the same way that a source-language reader might respond to the source text. For a text is a complex artifact that sustains meanings, values, and functions specific to its originary language and culture, and when translated this complexity is displaced by the creation of another text that comes to sustain meanings, values, and functions specific to a different language and culture. Any correspondence or approximation thus coincides with a radical transformation.

As a result, no translation can be understood as providing direct or unmediated access to its source text. Any text is only ever available through some sort of mediation, what Jacques Derrida calls an *inscription*, which discloses that the text has always already been positioned in a network of signification.[2] The mediation is most productively seen as a succession of interpretations in various forms and practices, media and institutions—even before a text becomes a source text that receives a translator's interpretation. The necessary mediation of interpretants allows any text to support multiple and conflicting interpretations as well as to give rise to many different translations. It also entails that the description, explanation, and evaluation of a translation is both enabled and constrained by the critic or reviewer's application of interpretants, which may or may not be consistent with those applied by the translator. Interpretation potentially releases an endless semiosis that is delimited by an interpretive occasion, an institutional site, a conjuncture of cultural forms and practices, and a historical moment—by, in other words, changing, interrelated, and mutually determining contexts of interpretation that can each lead to a different translation of the same source text, a condition of language use that Derrida terms *iterability*.[3]

In developing a hermeneutic model of translation that draws its key concepts from semiotics and poststructuralism, I am

deliberately setting aside the tradition of philosophical hermeneutics, particularly as exemplified by Martin Heidegger and
Hans-Georg Gadamer. Both Heidegger and Gadamer formulate
theories and methods of translation, but despite appreciable
advances, notably their attention to the intellectual and cultural
conditions of interpretation, their thinking ultimately devolves
into instrumentalism.

In "The Anaximander Fragment" (1946), for instance, Heidegger argues that any translation of this ancient text must avoid
the "Platonic and Aristotelian representations and concepts"
that "still guide the interpretation" of the early Greek thinkers.[4]
The "inadequate presuppositions" include such notions as that
Anaximander presents a "philosophy of nature" combined with
"inappropriate moralisms and legalisms," or that he addresses
specialized fields like the natural sciences, ethics, and law, or
that his "primitive outlook" represents the world "anthropo-
morphically" in "poetic expressions."[5] Heidegger insists that
these interpretive moves—all thematic interpretants in my
terminology—must be "consciously cast aside," whereupon
he proceeds to inscribe his own interpretation through his
translation.[6] He regards this interpretation, however, as the
essential meaning of the Greek fragment:

> Certainly we can translate γένεσις as origination; but we
> must think this originating as a movement which lets every
> emerging being abandon concealment and go forward into
> unconcealment. Certainly we can translate φθορά as passing
> away; but we must think this passing away as a going which
> in its turn abandons unconcealment, departing and with-
> drawing into concealment.[7]

Wohl können wir γένεσις durch Entstehen übersetzen; aber
wir müssen das Ent-stehen dabei denken als das Ent-gehen,

das jedes Entstehende der Verborgenheit ent-gehen und in das Unverborgene hervor-gehen läßt. Wohl können wir φθορά durch Vergehen übersetzen; aber wir müssen das Vergehen dabei denken als das Gehen, das dem Unverborgenen wieder ent-steht und in das Verborgene weg- und abgeht.[8]

According to the Liddell-Scott lexicon, which cites such sources as Aeschylus, Herodotus, and Plato, "γένεσις" (genesis) can be variously translated as "origin," "birth," "creation," and "coming into being," while "φθορά" (phthorá) encompasses "destruction," "death," "decay," and "ceasing to be."[9] Heidegger's German clearly acknowledges such meanings ("Enstehen," "Vergehen"), but he dismisses them in favor of "concealment" ("Verborgenheit") and "unconcealment" ("Unverborgenheit"), terms that refer to the notion of truth he formulated over the two decades that preceded his essay on Anaximander.[10] Heidegger invests his translation with a necessity ("must"/"müssen") that finally leads him to assert that it reflects the "truth of Being" ("Wahrheit des Seins").[11] In this way he construes his interpretation as a semantic invariant which he believes is reproduced in his German version. This invariant reduces the potential meanings of Anaximander's text, functioning as an inherent, unchanging essence that absurdly transforms the early Greek thinker into a promulgator of Heideggerian philosophy.

My aim is to put an end to such instrumentalist thinking in translation theory and commentary. It can be shown that instrumentalism is itself an interpretation that grossly oversimplifies translation practice, fostering an illusionism of immediate access to the source text which must be debunked and discarded. Instrumentalism constitutes a profoundly metaphysical kind of thinking that has stigmatized translation and prevented even the most sophisticated theorists and practitioners from advancing our knowledge and practice of it. A hermeneutic model, I argue, offers a more comprehensive and incisive understanding of translation that enables an appreciation not only of the creative and scholarly aspects of the translator's work, but also of the crucial role played by translation in the cultural and social institutions that shape human life. In my view, all translation, whether the genre of the source text is humanistic, pragmatic, or technical, is an interpretive act that necessarily entails ethical responsibilities and political commitments.

Although the focus of my intervention is the current situation, particularly in the United States, the application is global. The materials I use to build my arguments involve a variety of languages and cultures, including Arabic, Danish, French, Italian, German, Greek, Korean, Latin, and Spanish. My arguments, furthermore, possess a historical reach. The instrumental model first appears among Roman authors, particularly orators and rhetoricians like Cicero and Quintilian, and it is given a powerfully influential formulation by Jerome; the hermeneutic model, first appearing among German Romantic poets, critics, and translators like Goethe and the Schlegel brothers, is submitted to a philosophical examination by Friedrich Schleiermacher and subsequently reformulated by such twentieth-century thinkers as Heidegger and Derrida as well as the translation theorist Antoine Berman, although always at the risk of reintroducing instrumentalism.[12] While acknowledging these genealogies of the current situation, my project is strategic in emphasizing later transformations and consequences, both theoretical and practical: among Renaissance humanists and contemporary scholars of comparative literature, among structuralist and poststructuralist theorists, among translation researchers as well as translator trainers, among poets and poetry translators as well as film critics and subtitlers.

Method

I proceed by articulating the deeply embedded assumptions that make possible specific instances of translation theory, commentary, and practice, uncovering and interrogating not only the various discourses of instrumentalism, always culturally and historically situated, but also their preemption of or contradiction by a hermeneutic model. To perform these critical analyses I adapt to the field of translation studies a method that Michel Foucault calls "archaeological."[13]

A Foucauldian archaeology aims to articulate the "episteme" of a particular culture in a particular historical period, an "epistemological field" which Foucault describes as "the conditions of possibility of all knowledge, whether expressed in a theory or silently invested in a practice."[14] What I have termed a "model" of translation functions quite like an episteme: it is paradigmatic, consisting of fundamental relations between parameters and procedures that delimit what translation is and does, and it is generative, projecting various theoretical concepts and practical strategies that are specific to translation. Foucault imagined one episteme giving rise to a range of discursive formations, such as "the natural history, the economics, and the grammar of the Classical period," which construct domains of knowledge concerning living beings, wealth, and language.[15] The model I am imagining differs in its focus on a single domain, translation, shaping translation theory, commentary, and practice. Nonetheless, the model, like an episteme, establishes "rules of formation" that govern the discourses about translation across various fields and disciplines, including linguistics, modern languages, comparative literature, philosophy, and translation studies.[16]

Thus the instrumental model that defines translation as the reproduction of a source-text invariant generates the translation theorist Eugene Nida's concept of "equivalent effect," namely, "that the relationship between receptor and message should be substantially the same as that which existed between the original receptors and the message."[17] The equivalent effect is an invariant because it is assumed to be capable of replication regardless of the linguistic, cultural, and historical differences that distinguish between the source text and the translation as well as between the source and receiving situations. The concept of equivalent effect in turn generates the strategy of "compensation," defined by the linguist Keith Harvey as "a technique for making up for the loss of a source text effect by recreating a similar effect in the target text through means that are specific to the target language and/or the target text."[18] Compensation is an instrumentalist strategy because it assumes not simply that a source-text effect is an invariant, but also that its location and linguistic "means" can be changed in a translation without changing the significance or force that the effect carries in the source text. Although Harvey notes that "compensation does not necessarily involve systematic, one-to-one correspondence of individual source text and target text effects," he believes that the strategy remedies or supplies the "loss."[19] The instrumental model enables equivalent effect and compensation to be conceptualized and then deployed in studying, producing, and evaluating translations.

Similar connections occur between the hermeneutic model, on the one hand, and specific theoretical concepts and practical strategies, on the other. This model, defining translation as an interpretive act that varies the source text, generates the concept of mediation, namely, that the linguistic and cultural differences constituting that text are not immediately accessible in a translation but always reworked to be comprehended and affective in the translating culture. Hence Schleiermacher argues that the translator does not reproduce or transfer the source text itself but rather seeks to impart to the reader the same image [Bild], the same impression [Eindrukk] that he himself received thanks to his knowledge of the original language of the work as it was written, thus moving the reader to his own position, one in fact foreign [fremde] to him.[20]

If a translation creates an "image" and "impression" that remain "foreign" to the translator who then conveys them in all their foreignness to his reader, a translation elicits a rather different response compared to the one elicited by the source text from the source-language reader—that is, a reader for whom the source language would be familiar, if not native. An equivalent effect has been precluded. The concept of mediation in turn generates a strategy that aims to register or signal the foreignness of the source text, although indirectly, through the translating language. For Schleiermacher, this strategy not only adheres to the "turns and figures [Wendungen]" of the source text, its idiomatic and rhetorical features; it also cultivates a style that "departs from the quotidian [alltäglich]," using linguistic items that are not standard or not colloquial regardless of the language used in the source text.[21] Neither the source text nor the translating language escapes variation during the translation process.

Despite the appearance created by my examples, the connections between model, theory, and strategy should not be seen as one-to-one or exclusive. Although a certain consistency exists at the epistemic level, as Foucault indicates, "the episteme is not a motionless figure," but "a constantly moving set of articulations, shifts, and coincidences that are established, only to give rise to others."[22] A model of translation, similarly, can generate diverse theoretical concepts which can be realized by diverse practical strategies. Take the dichotomy between word-for-word vs. sense-for-sense translation: it articulates two rather different concepts of equivalence that both rest on the instrumental model. Word-for-word translation assumes a formal invariant, syntax or word order, projecting a strategy of close adherence to this feature of the source text, whereas sense-for-sense assumes a semantic invariant, an essential meaning, projecting a strategy that concentrates on this feature as opposed to individual words and their syntactic construction.

Originating in antiquity, the dichotomy was subsequently reformulated in different but equally instrumentalist terms. In the early modern period, for example, John Dryden expands it into a tripartite distinction: "Metaphrase, or turning an Authour word by word and Line by Line, from one Language into another"; "Paraphrase," where "his words are not so strictly follow'd as his sense, and that too is admitted to be amplyfied, but not alter'd"; and "Imitation," where a poet chooses a poet in a different language "not to Translate his words, or to be Confin'd to his Sense, but only to set him as a Patern, and to write, as he supposes, as the Authour would have done, had he liv'd in our Age and in our Country."[23] Dryden assumes that each strategy reproduces or transfers a source-text invariant, despite the departures that he is careful to note. He obviously finds nothing questionable in asserting that when a paraphrase is produced, the meaning of the source text can "be amplified, but not alter'd." Imitation might seem to be radically transformative, a practice of adaptation to the receiving situation rather than a translation. For Dryden, however, it can express the distinctive style of the source text, particularly when the imitator's poetic sensibility matches that of the foreign author. Thus it was only because Abraham Cowley possessed "a Genius so Elevated and unconfin'd" that his imitation of Pindar's odes could convey "so wild and ungovernable a Poet."[24] Two interrelated invariants would seem to be at stake in imitation, one formal (style), the other thematic (the author's sensibility).

Contradiction

A discursive formation is also "a space of multiple dissensions," which Foucault describes as "*intrinsic* oppositions" or "contradictions" that are grounded on the same episteme (hence "intrinsic" or "archaeologically *derived*").[25] These contradictions include "an *inadequation* of objects," "an *incompatibility* of concepts," or "an *exclusion* of theoretical options."[26] A model of translation, by the same token, can generate theoretical concepts that display such differences among themselves as to construct disparate objects of knowledge.

The instrumentalist dichotomy of word-for-word vs. sense-for-sense translation locates formal and semantic invariants at the level of word, phrase, or sentence, assuming that form and meaning are immediately accessible to the translator without aggressive interpretation. The linguists Basil Hatim and Ian Mason, in contrast, regard the translator's task as "piecing together these word-level and text-level meanings to form an overall textual strategy," and to this end they analyze both source texts and translations with an elaborate array of categories drawn from systemic-functional linguistics and pragmatics, what they call "basic standards of textuality" that include cohesion, implicature, politeness, register, and transitivity.[27] Here too the model is instrumental, the source text is thought to contain invariant features, but to access them the translator no longer works with mere words, phrases, or sentences. The invariants now consist of the linguistic and textual categories that serve as interpretive tools to formulate meanings. Compared to the ancient dichotomy, Hatim and Mason's linguistics-oriented discourse transforms entirely what a translated text is expected to reproduce or transfer.

Foucault acknowledges the possibility of "*extrinsic* contradictions that reflect the opposition between distinct discursive formations," each based on a different episteme (hence the contradictions are "extrinsic"), each formulating different theoretical concepts, each demarcating different domains of knowledge.[28] In the example he offers, "Linnaeus's fixism is contradicted by Darwin's evolutionism," since the former derives from the Classical episteme of identity and difference supporting taxonomic representation, whereas the latter derives from the "modern" episteme of dynamic functional system.[29] Extrinsic contradictions thus point to epistemological "breaks" or "ruptures," changes that reveal the emergence of a new episteme and require the archaeologist to "establish, between so many different changes, analogies and differences, hierarchies, complementarities, coincidences, and shifts: in short, to describe the dispersion of the discontinuities themselves."[30]

An archaeology of translation discourses can locate these discontinuities in individual texts. Although most accounts of translation are fundamentally either instrumentalist or hermeneutic, a particular account may rest on both models simultaneously, so that comments about theoretical concepts and practical strategies divulge a discontinuity at the level of their epistemological conditions. A work of translation theory or commentary enabled by one model might disclose the possibility that translation can be understood by the opposing model—and yet the work might suppress this possibility or leave it unexamined.

When Hatim and Mason describe their communicative approach, this sort of discontinuity tends to appear. Thus "translators," they assert, "seek to relay to a target reader what has already been communicated by a text producer and presented with varying degrees of explicitness in the text."[31] The very use of the word "relay" is instrumentalist: a metaphor drawn from information and communications technology, it signifies that a translation, like the transmission of an electronic signal, communicates the meaning of the source text without variation ("what has already been communicated by a text pro-ducer"). Yet if source-text meaning possesses "varying degrees of explicitness," the translator does not receive it directly, but must rather perform an interpretive act that determines the degrees to which meaning is explicit or implicit while inferring implicit meaning. A translator in a different time and place might interpret the source text differently, producing a different translation. Hatim and Mason would seem to agree when they define translation "as an act of communication which attempts to relay, across cultural and linguistic boundaries, another act of communication (which may have been intended for different purposes and different readers/hearers)."[32] The word "relay" again reveals their assumption of an instrumental model, but the parenthesis immediately subverts it: if the translation serves different purposes and addresses different audiences, variations in source-text form and meaning are inevitable not only when the translation is produced but also when it is received. Hatim and Mason neither formulate nor address the discontinuities in their accounts of translation.

The hermeneutic model can likewise meet with contradiction in a theoretical statement, especially when it incorporates an analysis of specific translations. On these occasions, an instru-mentalist comment may unexpectedly be made to skew the discussion away from the issue of interpretation—as if the mere presence of a translation were enough to invoke the assumption of a source-text invariant. André Lefevere, a translation theorist who specialized in Germanic studies and comparative literature, conceives of translation as a "refraction" that straddles two different cultural "systems," those in which the source text and the translation each originate under varying and possibly divergent "constraints" of "patronage" and "poetics," so that a translation represents a "compromise" between "the dominant constraints" of the two systems.[33] Lefevere's systemic approach assumes the hermeneutic model insofar as he defines a refraction as a text or practice that mediates a prior text. In this category he includes anthology editing, literary criticism and history, teaching, and theatrical production, as well as translation. "Writers and their work," he asserts, "are always understood and conceived against a certain background or, if you will, are refracted through a certain spectrum."[34] In this optics metaphor, the prism of patronage and poetics transforms the white light of the prior text into a continuum of colored light.

Yet the metaphor is questionable: according to the hermeneutic model, only the colors would be visible, never the white light in a pristine state. And as Lefevere's exposition unfolds, sure enough, any suggestion that a text is always already mediated is contradicted by an instrumentalist notion that direct access is possible. Thus immediately before the last sentence I quoted above he states that "a writer's work gains exposure and achieves influence mainly through 'misunderstandings and misconceptions,' or, to use a more neutral term, refractions," whereby he reduces refraction to error, a failure to comprehend the textual invariant that allows error to be discerned.[35] In the broader context of the entire essay, the quotation marks around "misunderstandings and misconceptions" function less as an attempt to put into question those negative terms than as an indication that Lefevere's concept of refraction sits uneasily on conflicting models of translation. The terms actually anticipate his instrumentalist censure of the translations he later examines, the first English versions of Brecht's *Mother Courage and Her Children* by H. R. Hays (1941) and Eric Bentley (1955).

"The main problem," in Lefevere's view, is the translators' effort "to accommodate Brecht's directness of diction to the poetics of the Broadway stage," specifically the musical.[36] He illustrates this "problem" with several scathing criticisms of the translations: he cites a "need to rhyme" that "leads to excessive padding, where the original is jarring and concrete"; "little of Brecht is left, but the seasons and sad reminiscence, so often *de rigueur* for Broadway, are certainly in evidence"; dramatic structure and stage directions "are two more features of the Brechtian poetics not seen as easily transferable from one system to another"; "a little emotion is added where emotion is too patently lacking."[37] When Lefevere analyzes the translations, he seamlessly segues into instrumentalism, assuming not only that Brecht's play contains formal and semantic invariants, but that they can be reproduced or transferred in a translation, and so any translation that omits or diminishes them should be faulted.

Lefevere momentarily flips back to the hermeneutic model when he allows for the possibility that "Brecht can be used in the service of a poetics diametrically opposed to his own, as in the Living Theater's production of *Antigone*."[38] The reference is to a 1968 production that staged Brecht's adaptation of Sophocles's play at Yale University. Given the Living Theater's commitment to modernist experimentalism based on Antonin Artaud's anarchist thinking, their production reflected a fairly elite cultural intervention, suggesting that Lefevere's preference expresses a snobbish antipathy toward a popular form like the Broadway musical.[39] If as a refraction a translation (or a theatrical production) is an interpretive act that inevitably transforms the source text, Lefevere should not be disparaging the Broadway poetics of the English translations for failing to reproduce Brecht's play. He should rather be considering how the musical genre nuances the significance of the German text and how that text in turn exposes an expressive potential in the genre that might not otherwise be perceived. He should, in other words, be exploring the interpretive angles constructed by the translation, conscious that his own interpretation is also a construction produced under institutional and cultural conditions that, by his own admission, do not favor the study of refractions such as translations.

The Epistemological Unconscious

The cases I have cited show that although a model of translation decisively shapes theoretical concepts and practical strategies, it is not deliberately chosen or implemented by a theorist, commentator, or translator. The model, like a Foucauldian episteme, amounts to "a *positive unconscious* of knowledge: a level that eludes the consciousness of the scientist and yet is part of scientific discourse."[40] As a result, a model of translation must be inferred from concepts and strategies, research projects and reviews, the formulation of translation problems and their resolution. Nowhere is a model presented with the detail or precision that I try to give it here because it remains deep-seated and unthought. Today, moreover, translation fosters varieties of anti-intellectualism that resist a searching critique of the epistemological conditions of theories and practices.[41] Translators, especially of literature, adopt a belletristic attitude that privileges the impressionistic and the intuitive, rarely articulating the concepts or interpretations that inform their work. Scholars succumb to disciplinary specializations that limit their thinking about translation to narrowly defined themes and methods, maintaining current orthodoxies and disregarding criticism from discourses that are marginal or originate in other disciplines.

All the same, terms and metaphors as well as discontinuities or contradictions can expose the underlying models in statements about translation. The instrumental model, in particular, has accumulated a battery of rhetorical moves. References to *preserving* or *losing* source-text features reveal instrumentalism because they imply that these features are invariants that ought to be reproduced or transferred in a translation. References to *truth* or *accuracy*, whether applied to interpretation or to translation, reveal instrumentalism because they imply unmediated access to source-text invariants, which are then made the criteria that determine error or inaccuracy. Metaphors that liken translation to changing clothes or painting a portrait, to metempsychosis, reincarnation, or transubstantiation, imply the intact transmission of a source-text essence. Certain metaphors, notably the analogy between translation and the performance of a dramatic text or a musical score, display a fundamental indeterminacy, capable of uses that are at times instrumental, at others hermeneutic.[42] The terms and metaphors are often employed so mechanically as to result in contradictory statements.

The classicist Emily Wilson, for example, in a profile where she discusses her 2017 translation of Homer's *Odyssey*, initially asserts that "all translations are interpretations" as her response to scholars who criticize her version because it is modernizing and therefore familiarizing.[43] Her assertion apparently adopts the hermeneutic model: it indicates a belief that a translation can never communicate the source text itself, only an interpretation of it, which can vary, moreover, with the historical moment when the translation is produced. Yet at the end she implicitly contradicts this view by suddenly referring to the inherent "truth" of the Greek text:

> "The fact that it's possible to translate the same lines a hundred different times and all of them are defensible in entirely different ways? That tells you something." But, Wilson added, with the firmness of someone making hard choices she believes in: "I want to be super responsible about my relationship to the Greek text. I want to be saying, after multiple different revisions: This is the best I can get toward the truth."[44]

Although Wilson does not explain the "something" that a hundred "defensible" versions might tell a reader, it would seem to bear out her earlier remark that translation is interpretation. Still, if the same poem can support so many translations, how can "*the* truth," a single, definitive truth, be located in the source text? Would not the truth make indefensible all translations that do not embody or approximate it by establishing an absolute standard that proves them wrong? Whatever Wilson believes the truth of the *Odyssey* to be, she has assumed the existence of an invariant, contained in the Greek text, and that becomes the goal she works "toward" achieving through successive revisions of her translation. Wilson obviously remains unaware of any logical inconsistency in her comments. So does Wyatt Mason, a literary translator himself, who authored the profile and unwittingly chose to emphasize Wilson's instrumentalism by concluding with it.

The fact is that the hermeneutic model, in understanding translation as variable interpretation, renders inadequate any appeal to the source text as the sole justification for a particular translation. The substantiating force of such an appeal must always give way to the relation that the translation establishes to the conditions that figure in its production and reception, conditions that are linguistic and cultural, institutional and social. With a text that has been retranslated as many times as the *Odyssey*, any justification for yet another version should distinguish it against previous interpretations and translations, ultimately considering their position in the hierarchy of values, beliefs, and social representations in the receiving situation. This hierarchy, a ranking according to cultural authority or prestige, matters for the viability of the interpretation inscribed in the source text, since it will inform readers' responses regardless of whether the translator takes it into account.[45] Those responses will of course vary according to diverse factors, personal as well as transindividual, but foremost among them is likely to be whether and how a retranslation conforms to or challenges dominant interpretations of the source text. By asserting that the Homeric text is the container of truth, Wilson has effectively suppressed these considerations.

Episteme vs. Model of Translation

Although adapting Foucault's method to translation studies reveals productive similarities between his project and mine, I do not want to lose sight of the equally illuminating differences. Models of translation as I conceive them are not in fact coterminous with his archeology of knowledge in Western culture. Foucault excavates the epistemes in three roughly approximate periods: resemblance from the sixteenth to the mid-seventeenth century (the Renaissance), representation from the mid-seventeenth to the end of the eighteenth century (the Classical period), and functional system from the nineteenth to the mid-twentieth century (the modern period). The models of translation possess a temporality that at once overlaps with and runs athwart Foucault's historical divisions. Instrumentalism can be perceived in statements about translation from antiquity straight through to the present, although during the periods that Foucault has marked out these statements do disclose the operation of the concurrent epistemes. The hermeneutic model, emerging during the late eighteenth and early nineteenth centuries and persisting in statements about translation into the present, reflects the modern episteme which foregrounds the conditions that enable and constrain knowledge. The different temporalities suggest that although a model of translation can function within the conceptual parameters demarcated by an episteme, model and episteme are distinct categories, they have no necessary connection to one another, and they follow different trajectories of development. The model of translation seems in fact to expose a limitation in Foucault's concept of the episteme, a blind spot that points to another epistemological level beneath the consciously executed work in discursive formations—or at least beneath the discourses that determine the knowledge and practice of translation.

To elucidate this peculiar disjunction, consider a metaphor that recurs in instrumentalist statements across millennia. Roman commentators draw an analogy between clothing and language as a vehicle for thought, and by the sixteenth century it is routinely applied to translation, positing a semantic invariant as the source-text body which the translator clothes in corresponding language from the receiving situation.[46] George Chapman relies on this metaphor in prefacing his 1611 translation of the *Iliad*, where "every knowing and judiciall" translator is said to eschew word-for-word equivalence, taking source-text "sentences" as the unit of translation, focusing on their meanings or "the materiall things" they signify, and choosing "apt" translating language "to clothe and adorne them":

> it is the part of every knowing and judiciall interpreter not to follow the number and order of words but the materiall things themselves, and sentences to weigh diligently, and to clothe and adorne them with words and such a stile and forme of Oration as are most apt for the language into which they are converted.[47]

Chapman's discourse is immersed in the instrumentalist treatises of ancient commentators like Cicero and Quintilian. They distinguish between *res* (things) and *verba* (words) in discussing the relation between meaning and language, and they recommend sense-for-sense equivalence in translations designed to train the orator, contrasting their approach with the grammarian's emphasis on word-for-word renderings.[48] Hence Chapman refers to a translation as an "Oration," a rhetorical performance, and he employs revealing Latinisms, virtual calques of words used by Cicero in *De optimo genere oratorum* (46 BCE; On the

Best Kind of Orators), calling the translator an "interpreter" (Cicero's term is "interpres") and describing translation as a process by which the source text is "converted" (Cicero uses "converti") into the translating language.[49]

Yet in addition to sharing the instrumentalism of his ancient authorities, Chapman's metaphorical account of translation can also be described as governed by the Renaissance episteme of resemblance. He imagines an unbroken chain of similitudes that extends from "the materiall things" of the source text to the source-language "sentences" that express those "things" to the translating-language "words" that with "such a stile and forme" are able to "clothe and adorne" the source-text "things" and "sentences." The word "apt" not only makes explicit the correspondence between source and translating languages, but also continues the clothing metaphor by working as a pun: it indicates language that is both "fitting" or "appropriate" and "fitted" like a garment.[50]

The chain of similitudes is deepened by the polysemous pronouns. "Them" can encompass both "the materiall things" and "sentences," and "they" can denote features of both the source text ("the materiall things" and "sentences") and the translation ("words," "stile and forme"). Consequently, the convoluted syntax of Chapman's assertion constructs a dense signification of three translation processes that mirror each other: one process is situated within the source text ("the materiall things" are "converted" into "sentences" which are the "language" that is "most apt" for those "things"); another process unfolds within the translation itself (the translator chooses "words and such a stile and forme" that are "most apt" for the translating "language into which they are converted" or in which their function is changed to be effective as a translation);[51] and yet another process occurs between the source text and the translation ("the materiall things" and their "sentences" are "converted"

into the translating "language" that is "most apt" for them).
Supported by the Renaissance episteme, Foucault notes, "the
nature of things, their coexistence, the way in which they are
linked together and communicate is nothing other than their
resemblance," whereby "signs and similitudes were wrapped
around one another in an endless spiral."[52] Resemblance in effect
historicizes Chapman's instrumentalist discourse on translation
by producing period-specific formulations.

Nonetheless, instrumentalism originates long before the
Renaissance and continues long past it, revealing the operation
of changing epistemological conditions. The Classical episteme
of representation significantly redefines the clothing metaphor
for translation. In his *Essay on the Principles of Translation* (1791), a
compendium of topoi that accumulated during the seventeenth
and eighteenth centuries, Alexander Fraser Tytler observes
that "a good translator must be able to discover at once the true
character of his author's style," explaining that "if a translator
fail in this discernment, and want this capacity let him be ever
so thoroughly master of the sense of his author, he will present
him through a distorting medium, or exhibit him often in a
garb that is unsuitable to his character."[53]

The "style" of the source text constitutes a formal invariant
available to the translator's immediate "discernment" without the intervention of any interpretive labor. The translation,
accordingly, is a "medium" that can "present" this invariant
clearly, without any "distorting" obstruction, so that in applying
the clothing metaphor Tytler assumes the "garb" of the translating language to be effectively invisible—unless the translator
has failed to reproduce or transfer the style. This conception of
language and translation reflects the Classical episteme where,
Foucault points out, "the signifying element has no content, no
function, and no determination other than what it represents:
it is entirely ordered upon and transparent to it."[54]

A clothing analogy likewise epitomizes the instrumentalism of Walter Benjamin's essay, "The Translator's Task" (1923), although here the episteme not only underpins but also complicates Benjamin's discourse. Foucault remarks that the modern episteme of functional system treats the individual word as belonging to "a grammatical totality which, in relation to the word, is primary, fundamental, and determining," giving rise to "the isolation of the Indo-European languages, the constitution of a comparative grammar, the study of inflections, the formulation of the laws of vowel gradation and consonantal changes—in short, the whole body of philological work accomplished by Grimm, Schlegel, Rask, and Bopp."[55] The same episteme that generates nineteenth-century philology underlies Benjamin's assertion that "the kinship of languages manifests itself in translation," but he joins this systemic notion to a messianic theology and hence any "historical kinship" becomes "suprahistorical" and eschatological.[56] In Benjamin's account, the lexical and syntactical differences that constitute languages make them "mutually exclusive," but they "complement each other in their intentions" to "signify one and the same thing," so that the translator's work on the source text betokens "the totality of their mutually complementary intentions: pure language"—which, however, is fully revealed only when "they reach the messianic end of their history."[57]

Benjamin's particular instrumentalism manifests the historical tendency of the modern episteme but winds up contradicting it. Imagining "the inner life of language and its works" as "one of the most powerful and fruitful historical processes," he questions the "traditional theory of translation," specifically the idea of "conveying the form and sense of the original as accurately as possible"; linguistic development, he argues, ensures that "just as the tone and significance of great literary works are completely transformed over the centuries, the translator's native language is also transformed."[58] Yet these transformations do not in any way qualify Benjamin's insistence that the translator confronts a number of invariants. The source text contains what he variously calls a "message," "information," "content," or "sense" ("Mitteilung," "Aussage," "Inhalt," "Sinn"), a semantic invariant which can submit to "transmission," "communication," or "reproduction" in a translation, but which he regards as "inessential" and therefore disparages as not "genuine."[59] The source text also contains a formal invariant, the "unity" of "literary language" and "content," an organic "relation" that Benjamin likens to "a fruit and its skin" and describes as "not translatable."[60] The most important invariant is pure language, which does not inhere in the formal and semantic features of the source text or the translation but instead transcends them and is therefore untranslatable, as figured in the analogy of the "royal mantle."[61] Benjamin's instrumentalist discourse shows quite clearly that claims of translatability or untranslatability require the assumption of an invariant:

> One can extract from a translation as much communicable information as one wishes, and this much can be translated; but the element toward which the genuine translator's efforts are directed remains out of reach. It is not translatable, like the literary language of the original, because the relation between content and language in the original is entirely different from that in the translation. If in the original, content and language constitute a certain unity, like that between a fruit and its skin, the language of a translation surrounds its content, as if with the broad folds of a royal mantle. For translation indicates a higher language than its own and thereby remains inadequate, violent, and alien with respect to its own content.[62]

Benjamin's reference to "broad folds" indicates that the translating language can signify two invariants simultaneously, even if differently and somewhat imperfectly. The "information" or "content" contained in a translation comes from the translatable part of the source text, the semantic invariant to which most translators try to maintain a correspondence. The "higher" or pure language, however, the invariant sought by the "genuine" translator, makes the translation "inadequate, violent, and alien" in relation to its content because pure language becomes perceptible only through close adherence to source-text "syntax," through "word-for-word translation," which "completely thwarts the reproduction of the sense and threatens to lead directly to incomprehensibility."[63] The analogy likens pure language to the body of a king, although given the messianism that Benjamin assigns to that notion, the kingship can only be sacral. Just as the broad folds of the royal mantle symbolize the king's divinely ordained authority, the "literalness" of the translating language results in a loose or imprecise signification of meaning because it symbolizes "the true language," where "truth" is described as unmediated "revelation" ("Offenbarung") comparable to Holy Scriptures.[64]

Benjamin's instrumentalism thus leads to a mystical transcendence of language as a material medium, the very category that is central to the philological work buttressed by the modern episteme. "True translation," he asserts, "is transparent" like the "interlinear version" of the Bible, where "the text belongs immediately to truth or doctrine, without the mediation of sense."[65] In formulating this view, Benjamin suppresses the conceptual scaffolding that supports his own theoretical speculation on language, what has been described as "a peculiar amalgam of Kantian 'mysticism,' Early Romanticism (Schlegel and Novalis), Hölderlin's poetry, Hamann's aphorisms, and the Kabbalah."[66] Nonetheless, there can be no doubt that pure language, whether released by a translator or perceived by a reader, entails an interpretive act that inscribes a set of quintessentially theological concepts through translation.

In the discourse driving my polemic, the modern episteme that generated the hermeneutic model of translation among Romantic thinkers like Schleiermacher has been modified by semiotics and poststructuralism, incorporating concepts of language, textuality, and interpretation that signal an epistemic shift toward postmodernism. This uneasy synthesis permits the critical scrutiny that ferrets out instrumentalist assumptions in diverse statements on translation, bringing the two competing models to consciousness while leaving unexplored or simply unthought the possibility of other theoretical concepts and practical strategies. In questioning instrumentalist thinking about translation, I want to avoid any reinstatement of its essentialism by remaining mindful of the limitations of my own discourse. Hence my universalist claims—namely, that all translation is an interpretive act, and that the hermeneutic model offers the most comprehensive and incisive understanding of translation—these claims must be counterbalanced by a recognition of their actual contingency: they derive from, in order to intervene against, the contemporary situation of translation theory and commentary, where the instrumental model enjoys such dominance as to marginalize the hermeneutic approach. Foucault describes the sort of critique I am pursuing as

genealogical in its design and archaeological in its method. Archaeological—and not transcendental—in the sense that it will not seek to identify the universal structures of all knowledge or of all possible moral action, but will seek to treat the instances of discourse that articulate what we think, say, and do as so many historical events. And this critique will be genealogical in the sense that it will not deduce from the form of what we are what is impossible for us to do and to know; but it will separate out, from the contingency that has made us what we are, the possibility of no longer being, doing, or thinking what we are, do, or think.[67]

Institutional Sites: Professional Translation

A critique with these aims requires an examination of the institutions in which discourses exert their power in constructing identity, knowledge, and action. In the case of my project, the key institutional sites, those where translations are produced and circulated, house discursive forms and practices governed by models of translation. How, I want to ask, does the instrumental model affect the way that translation is understood and evaluated not only by translators and publishers, but also by academics who use translations in their research and teaching or who study and teach it? How does the idea that translation is an interpretive act get formulated or suppressed by these agents? To introduce this line of inquiry and illustrate how it is pursued in the chapters that follow, I will consider three institutional sites: the profession of literary translation, including its connection with the publishing industry; the academic discipline of modern languages and literatures; and translation studies, an emerging cross-disciplinary field in the academy which includes translation research and translator training.

Mark Polizzotti can be taken as representative not only of professional literary translators who work on a freelance basis but also of editors of translations based in publishing houses. Since the early 1980s he has produced over fifty English translations of French texts, fiction as well as nonfiction, mainly novels and art criticism. His work has been issued by a wide range of publishers, including large commercial conglomerates (Houghton Mifflin Harcourt, Penguin), small- to-midsize firms (Archipelago, City Lights, Dalkey Archive, New Directions, the

New Press, Other Press, Semiotext(e)), and university presses (Minnesota, Nebraska, Yale). At the same time, Polizzotti has worked as an in-house editor for several trade publishers where he has acquired translation rights and edited translations: Random House (1983–1985), Grove Weidenfeld (1985–1990), and David R. Godine (1993–1999). More recently, he has overseen the publishing programs at the Museum of Fine Arts in Boston (1999–2010) and the Metropolitan Museum of Art in New York (since 2010) where he has edited and translated material for exhibition catalogues.[68] He has also been a member of the selection committee for "French Voices," a program administered by the French American Cultural Exchange and the French Embassy to award publishing subventions that support English translations of French texts.[69] Since 2011 he has expressed his views on translation in various essays and interviews which he subsequently developed into a book-length "translation manifesto," entitled *Sympathy for the Traitor* (2018).

Polizzotti's text does not offer a coherently argued account of translation substantiated by exhaustive research, but rather a string of largely unexplained assertions couched in overstatement, metaphor, and cliché. He insists that he is presenting "an 'antitheory,' or perhaps just a common-sense approach," which leads him to draw a distinction between theory and practice that is not merely naïve but staunchly anti-intellectual: "no theory or dogma," he states at the outset, "can replace the translator's work of grappling with the text on its own terms, of devising an appropriate strategy."[70] He seems entirely unaware that no translation strategy can be devised except on the basis of theoretical assumptions about writing and translation as well as linguistic and cultural differences, or that his own practical orientation can be described as dogmatic. His manifesto, not surprisingly, is riddled with contradictions that display how the instrumental model cuts off thinking about translation among translators and publishers.

At points, Polizzotti does seem to assume the hermeneutic model. He wants to "think of the source text not as a defined, monolithic whole that can never be replicated adequately, but rather as a zone of energy, always in flux, endlessly prone to different assimilations and interpretations."[71] This statement avoids an essentialist notion of the source text ("a defined, monolithic whole" that is untranslatable) and implicitly regards translation as a variable interpretation. Yet statements to the contrary begin to proliferate, and the instrumental model quickly becomes an overriding assumption. Although Polizzotti acknowledges "the conviction" among many readers that "reading an author in translation is not *really* reading him at all," he contends that "if the translation is performed well, we will have read the essence of what the author meant us to read."[72] Here he posits a metaphysical "essence" contained in the source text, an invariant that realizes authorial intention and can be fully reproduced or transferred in a translation.

For Polizzotti, the invariant somehow remains intact even when the translator revises the source text. "Judicious restructuring," he believes, "brings you closer to the author's desired effect than a close parallel."[73] He speaks of "being sufficiently attuned to each nuance to divine where the author was going" and yet of "constantly interrogating the text, trying to get behind it and adapting when necessary."[74] If translation involves "constantly interrogating" the source text to detect "where the author was going," much more is happening than the translator's "being sufficiently attuned." The author's intention appears not to be self-evident, so the translator must interpret the source text to infer it and then resort to manipulation ("adapting") to make the translation correspond to that interpretation—which, however, Polizzotti understands as equivalent to the author's intention.

His instrumentalism renders invisible this complicated process of mediation, causing him to adopt the misguided belief that no substantial difference exists between his translations and the source texts they translate.

Polizzotti's manifesto is weakest whenever he tries to account for the interpretations that translators inscribe in their source texts. He quotes a passage from surrealist Paul Éluard's 1930 imitation of psychopathological language and juxtaposes it to two English versions, one by Richard Howard (1965), which uses current standard English in a conversational register, the other by Samuel Beckett (1932), which uses early modern pronouns in a more formal register. Polizzotti praises Howard's version lukewarmly, calling it "a rather jocular interpretation, as if Éluard were being read by Cary Grant," while reserving his enthusiasm for Beckett's: "by transposing the discourse of a general paralytic from 1930 into the heraldic idiom of courtly love lyrics, Beckett has come closer to preserving the essence of Éluard's feverish entreaty than Howard, even though Howard actually hews closer to the strict meaning of the original."[75]

With each translation Polizzotti has interestingly isolated formal interpretants, stylistic features linked to genres and media, which have a thematic force in inscribing meanings. But why Beckett's intertext ("courtly love lyrics" signaled by archaisms like "thou") should be preferred to Howard's intersemiotic affiliation (phrases like "my great big adorable girl" evoking Hollywood actor Cary Grant) remains questionable. After all, a screwball comedy like Howard Hawks's *Bringing Up Baby* (1938), which starred Grant, has been described as possessing "elements of surrealism" so that the actor's "interpretation" might be seen as appropriate for translating Éluard's text.[76] Because Polizzotti's discourse is so resolutely instrumentalist, concerned with "preserving the essence" of the source text, he ignores issues that could help to make sense of the differences between the two versions, such as connections they might have to translation practices in their historical moments or to the translators' other work as well as the fact that Howard is retranslating the French text after Beckett and might be engaged in one-upmanship. Polizzotti does not even mention the publication dates of the translations. Hence he cannot give an illuminating explanation of their effects or a persuasive justification of his evaluation, which seems purely arbitrary, mere personal preference. It will not do to argue that Beckett reproduces "Éluard's feverish entreaty" whereas Howard does not: that very term is Polizzotti's interpretation; the French text can support other, different readings.

Whenever Polizzotti raises the question of "how to judge a translation," he repeatedly mentions "how convincing it is," but this quality is never defined.[77] It seems to amount to how seamlessly the translator can inscribe his interpretation in a source text, or how effectively he can create the illusion of transparency that allows the translation to pass for the source text when in fact the translation process opens up significant differences between them.[78] Although Polizzotti wields considerable power in the publishing industry, receiving many commissions to translate French texts, editing many translations, and influencing funding decisions, he is unable—or just refuses—to provide a cogent account of translation that engages and educates readers, choosing instead to mystify the conditions of his work.

Institutional Sites: The Academy

Michael J. McGrath can serve to represent the academic specialist in modern languages and literatures who evaluates and edits English translations of works in his field. A professor of Hispanic Studies at Georgia Southern University since 2000, McGrath specializes in early modern Spanish literature and culture. He has published three research monographs, which include *Religious Celebrations in Segovia, 1577–1697* (2002) and *Teatro y fiesta en la ciudad de Segovia (siglos XVIII y XIX)* (2015). He has edited festschrifts for Hispanists who were former teachers of his at the University of Kentucky, John Jay Allen (2005) and Edward F. Stanton (2016), and he has produced annotated editions of Spanish texts intended especially for American students, including the work of Calderón (2003, 2013) and Cervantes (2008). McGrath has published most of his books with imprints of LinguaText, a small press founded in 1974 by the University of Delaware Hispanist Tom Lathrop to bring out foreign-language textbooks and related materials. McGrath himself edits one imprint at LinguaText, Juan de la Cuesta Hispanic Monographs, where he oversees a series of English translations that includes canonical authors such as Benito Pérez Galdós, Ramón María Valle-Inclán, and Miguel Delibes. The translators are, like McGrath, academic specialists in Spanish literature and culture.

Perhaps the most noticeable aspect of McGrath's work, both his research and his editing, is its high degree of specialization, defined not only by the Spanish language, but also by particular historical periods, particular cultural themes and practices, even a particular city in Spain. These parameters are further circumscribed by a field-specific network of colleagues and contributors, imprints and journals. The narrowness of this specialization motivated McGrath's 2008 article for the *Bulletin of the Cervantes Society of America* in which he criticized English translations of Cervantes's *Don Quixote*, following the example set by John Jay Allen some thirty years before.[79] McGrath examines eight versions published between 1949 and 2007, while Allen examines seven dating from roughly the seventeenth to the mid-twentieth centuries. Although both scholars indicate "errors," "distortions," and "losses" in the translations, McGrath goes beyond Allen in asserting a sense of academic territoriality. Not only does McGrath assign the enormous value to the source text that might be expected of a period specialist presiding over a canon—it possesses "genius" for him—but he explicitly states that only translators who are "scholars of Spain's Golden Age, and especially Cervantine literature," can offer "a true appreciation of the novel."[80] These translators include Tom Lathrop, who published his 2007 version of *Don Quixote* with LinguaText before it appeared as a mass-market paperback with Signet Classics in 2011, extending the circulation of his scholarly version into popular readerships.

McGrath's critical commentary on the translations validates the cultural authority of the Hispanist, although the validation requires that his commentary assume the instrumental model. He observes, for example, that to translate "adarga" at the beginning of *Don Quixote* both Samuel Putnam (1949) and Walter Starkie (1964) use "buckler" as opposed to the more prevalent choice of "shield," and he concludes that only "Putnam and Starkie remain loyal to the original meaning of the [Spanish] word" whereas the other translators introduce a "variation" or "distortion" by using "a more general term with which English speakers are more apt to identify."[81] McGrath bases his definition of "buckler" ("a shield that fastens to the arm") on the *Diccionario de autoridades*, an eighteenth-century lexicon that takes its illustrative quotations from Spanish authors of the sixteenth and seventeenth centuries, including Cervantes.[82] To document his evaluation of the translations, McGrath cites the first part of the entry for "adarga" (my English version below aims to maintain a semantic correspondence):

Cierto género de escudo compuesto de duplicados cueros, engrudados, y cosidos unos con otros, de figura quasi ovál, y algunos de la de un corazón: por la parte interior tiene en el medio dos asas, la priméra entra en el brazo izquierdo, y la segunda se empuña con la mano.

A certain kind of shield made of two identical pieces of leather, pasted, and sewn together, almost oval in form, although some are heart-shaped: on the inside it has two handles, the first slips over the left arm, and the second is grasped by the hand.

McGrath's instrumentalism makes his evaluation appear self-evident: to him, the Spanish text simply contains a semantic invariant, "the original meaning" of "adarga," and the mere citation of a dictionary is sufficient to prove that. But McGrath has actually performed a rather complicated interpretive act that preempts other, equally viable interpretations. He has determined, first, that the individual word should be taken as the unit of translation—in contrast to such other possible units as the sentence or the paragraph and regardless of what unit the translator may have chosen. In the same stroke, McGrath has made a second determination, namely, that the relation of equivalence between the source text and the translation should be established between individual words—in contrast not only to other linguistic items or textual divisions, but also to such other possible features of literary form as style, point of view, or genre. Again, regardless of the translator's decisions. McGrath has thus applied two formal interpretants in conjunction with a thematic one: the *Diccionario de autoridades*, which he has employed to fix the meaning of "adarga."

The use of this reference work is directly linked to the institutional site that supports McGrath's authority: the academy. Known primarily to academic specialists, the *Diccionario de autoridades* allows him to exclude other dictionaries that define the Spanish word less elaborately as "oval leather shield," "(oval) shield," and "leather shield."[83] It also allows him to invoke what

Frank Kermode calls the "hermeneutic restrictions" imposed by academic institutions, the decision as to what means of interpretation are permissible.[84] In preferring "buckler" over "shield," furthermore, McGrath is applying yet another formal interpretant, the requirement that "translators must aspire to preserve the archaic style in which the characters speak," although he seems oblivious of the fact that for Cervantes and his contemporaries "adarga" was current, not archaic, and so to choose an archaism like "buckler" or to apply an archaizing strategy throughout cannot precisely be said to present "a true appreciation of the novel" in the twentieth or twenty-first centuries.[85]

Echoing John Jay Allen's suspicion of translations, McGrath asserts that "literary scholarship runs the risk of being skewed as a result of the translator's inability to capture the text's original meaning."[86] Yet at least Allen was aware of "the notorious difficulty in establishing the locus of value in *Don Quixote*," that the Spanish text, in other words, contains interpretive cruxes that are not so easily resolved, particularly in translation.[87] Through an instrumentalist criticism of translations, McGrath wishes to control the interpretations of Cervantes's novel by reserving it for Hispanists and stigmatizing interpretive possibilities that do not conform to prevalent academic standards, but that might appeal to readerships outside of the academy.

In the field of translation studies, Brian Mossop's work is representative of a dominant tendency that looks to current practices in the translation industry to guide academic research and training. Mossop took a master's degree in linguistics at the University of Toronto but stopped short of completing his doctoral dissertation in order to translate professionally. Between 1974 and 2014, he worked as a salaried French-to-English translator in Toronto, first in the Translation Bureau of the Secretary of State of Canada, then in the Department of Public Works and Government Services. Many of the texts he translated fell into scientific fields, including ecology, forestry, and meteorology; others were related to public policy issues such as transportation, penitentiaries, immigration, and refugees. In the 1970s he began to train government translators, and in 1980 he became a part-time instructor in the School of Translation at Glendon College of York University, teaching such topics as the translation of specialized texts, revising and editing, and translation theory. He is the author of the manual, *Revising and Editing for Translators* (2001), now in its fourth edition, as well as some fifty articles and reviews in edited volumes and in refereed journals like *Meta: Journal des traducteurs*, *Perspectives: Studies in Translatology*, *Target: International Journal of Translation Studies*, and *The Translator*.

The close relationship between translation practice, teaching, and research in Mossop's career is not unusual. It can be considered the main motivation for his 2017 "position paper" in which he argues, largely on the basis of his forty-year experience as a government translator and trainer of translators, that "the invariance-oriented mental stance of most producers in the translation industry" should be "a central object of translation studies."[88] By "invariance-orientation" Mossop means that "the basic mental orientation" of most translators worldwide "is to strive for invariance of meaning and to minimize deliberate variance."[89] Although his assumption of the instrumental model seems clear enough, foregrounding the reproduction of a semantic invariant, his exposition is confused and winds up not only suppressing a hermeneutic understanding of translation but also minimizing the various conditions—linguistic and cultural, institutional and social—that figure in the production and reception of translations.

The confusion appears as so many blurred distinctions, if not outright contradictions. Mossop asserts that his notion of invariance emphasizes "intention rather than outcome" because some degree of variation inevitably occurs in translation; hence the sign of invariance is "not so much the presence of a large number of semantic correspondences between source text and translation" as "rather the social circumstances of production," including "what the commissioner expects" or "the practicalities of translating for clients who have particular purposes."[90] Yet these "circumstances" and "purposes," even if seen as part of the translator's intention, cannot be called strictly "mental": they bear on "outcome" since they ensure that the invariance-oriented translator is constrained by the effect produced by the translation or the function it is intended to serve. Thus any distinction between intention and outcome has collapsed, and the invariant would seem to have shifted from meaning to effect or function. Mossop explains: "a few deliberate changes in meaning here and there in a text do play an essential role, to make the output useable."[91]

Nonetheless, the effect or function of a translation cannot be treated as a reliable criterion by which to establish or measure invariance. For it too can vary, depending on the context of interpretation in which the translation is produced or used, a context that is institutional or social. This point has eluded Mossop. He believes that a client's purpose can stabilize "a translator's concept of meaning sameness" by eliminating any "quirkiness": "if you are translating a drug information sheet for a pharmaceutical company," he states, "you will avoid fanciful interpretations and even minor omissions."[92] But what if the translator does avoid these moves and the translation becomes evidence in a legal suit against the pharmaceutical company? The translator's intention to maintain semantic invariance may conceivably come to serve purposes or interests that actually oppose those of the client's. Function can be applied as a thematic interpretant in producing or using a translation, but its significance will change with different institutional conditions.

Similar confusions arise when Mossop insinuates the idea that invariance-oriented translation is an interpretive act. The intention of most translators, he indicates, is "to convey as much as possible their interpretation of the source text," admitting that "actually achieving a high degree of meaning invariance is quite difficult, and various third parties (a reviser, a translation teacher or scholar, a bilingual user functioning as a critic) may disagree about whether it has been achieved."[93] Here translation seems to involve variable interpretation: a source text can support various degrees of semantic correspondence, however limited or inexact a third party may judge them to be. Yet when Mossop describes the translation process, including his own, his remarks are undoubtedly instrumentalist. He declares that "teasing out the source's precise meaning and then capturing it as quickly as possible in the other language is what I . . . have found so interesting about the act of translating"; for him, translation is the "creation of equivalence" in the sense of "preserving meaning."[94] In such statements, meaning is assumed to be an unchanging essence inherent in the source text and therefore undetermined by an interpretant like the function of the translation.

The instrumentalism that underpins Mossop's thinking stems from his conservative reaction against theoretical developments in translation studies. He complains that "theoretical writing does tend to focus rather obsessively these days on difference rather than sameness," and he accounts for this tendency by observing that the topic of invariance "was largely abandoned in the 1980s, when the focus shifted to how translations differ from their sources in order to communicate with future users in target-language cultures—a shift that turned out to fit nicely with the cultural keyword 'diversity.'"[95] Mossop seems to have in mind the emergence of poststructuralism as a critical orthodoxy in the humanities during the 1980s, when concepts of translation as a transformative practice were widely accepted and linked to forms of ideological critique.[96] Beyond his vague complaints, however, he does not engage with what he calls "variance-oriented translation theory," a term that does not suggest any understanding of the theoretical discourses he opposes.[97]

The hermeneutic model as I have formulated it does not require or recommend that the translator deliberately vary the source text. It rather conceives of translation as fundamentally variable interpretation, but it can nonetheless encompass different concepts of equivalence, including semantic correspondence and stylistic approximation. As a result, the hermeneutic model can only question any uncritical acceptance of invariance, whether that orientation derives from the translation industry or describes the current practices of professional translators. Mossop's position paper implies, regrettably, that his translation practice, teaching, and research have long sought to maintain the status quo in translation simply by taking it for granted.

Desiring-Machine

In choosing START/STOP as the title of this introduction, I am not so much imposing a mechanistic metaphor for reading as invoking Gilles Deleuze and Félix Guattari's concept of the "desiring-machine" or "machinic assemblage."[98] I see this book functioning as a device of "desiring-production" in their sense, producing in you, my reader, the will to critique a model that has been so deeply entrenched in thinking about translation for so long as to be unconscious, knee-jerk, rote. The difficulty or apparent inability to criticize instrumentalism means that coolly detached reasoning is not enough to be persuasive, this model is heavily cathected with desire, and the provocation of polemic has become necessary to release and redirect it.

The critical readings that accompany the exposition of

my method have already started the project of derailing the continuing dominance of instrumentalism, of stopping its operation and replacing it with translation research and practice that are radically hermeneutic. Our point of departure is the acknowledgment that the source text comes to the translation process always already mediated, capable of supporting multiple and conflicting interpretations which are limited only by the institutions where a translation is produced and circulated. "Desiring-machines," write Deleuze and Guattari, "function within social machines" that repress the essentially "explosive" force of desire, its capacity to "deterritorialize" institutionalized practices: "there is no desiring-machine capable of being assembled without demolishing entire social sectors."[99] To change thinking about translation is to change the institutions that house the various forms and practices of cultural production. The question I pose to you, then, is: Are you ready to examine how you think about translation—and to change it?

The "contra" in my title is intended to evoke patristic controversy in late antiquity when translation was so central to scholarship as to figure in heated discussion. Academia around the world urgently needs to restore that centrality, to recognize that translation lies at the core, not only of humanistic study and research, but also of the geopolitical economy that structures social relations today—provided that translation is conceived and practiced as an ethically charged and politically engaged act of interpretation.

Where is your desire?

1

Hijacking Translation

Uneven Developments

Academia is slow to change. The snag, as Pierre Bourdieu observed, is resistance to new ideas which favors those that currently enjoy authority in a particular field.[1] Academics harbor an anti-intellectualism, ironically, bred by the splintering of intellectual labor into so many institutional compartments. To specialize, however productive the yield in quantity and depth of knowledge, is to clap on a set of blinders.

Take the field of comparative literature. It originated in late nineteenth-century Europe, and from the 1950s onward it was firmly established in the United States, invigorated by the contributions of European émigré scholars and housed in departments and programs at many academic institutions. By 1975 a total of 150 schools offered degrees or concentrations on both the undergraduate and graduate levels; currently that figure stands at 187.[2] Despite this remarkable growth, comparatists took more than a century to recognize that the field was grounded on fundamentally Eurocentric and nationalist assumptions.

During this period, the notion of comparing literatures amounted in most cases to a methodology that contained three critical moves. Resemblances were located among forms and themes from a canon of European works read in their original languages; differences were made intelligible in terms of the national languages, traditions, and cultures in which those works were rooted; more sweeping generalizations, whether transnational or universal, might ultimately be ventured, depending on the comparatist's assumptions about literature, society, or humanity. Erich Auerbach's magisterial *Mimesis* (1946), a *locus classicus* for this methodology, surveys "the literary representation of reality in European culture" from antiquity to the twentieth century, explicitly excluding the "consideration" of "foreign influences" ("fremde Einwirkungen") as "not necessary" (where "foreign" means transnational as well as non-European).[3] Comparatists were expected to master a minimum of four European languages, including English, regardless of the fact that they increasingly came to rely on translations in their research and teaching. Not until the early 1990s, when the American Comparative Literature Association (ACLA) commissioned Charles Bernheimer to submit a committee-drafted "Report on Standards," did the field publicly confront its long exclusion of non-European cultures as well as the stigma it had attached to translation. The 1993 Bernheimer report, which was published with sixteen "responses" and "position papers," aimed to bring comparative literature in line with what were then perceived as "progressive tendencies in literary studies, toward a multicultural, global, and interdisciplinary curriculum," encompassing developments in literary and cultural theory, cultural studies, and film studies and treating elite literature as one among an array of cultural forms and practices.[4]

Yet, despite the controversy provoked by the Bernheimer report, not much changed. Postcolonial theory emerged, decades after the militant anticolonial movements, amid an already expanded canon that included African, Asian, and Latin American literatures. By the 1990s this expansion had been institutionalized in myriad courses, publications, conferences, and professorships. Nonetheless, canons are by definition exclusionary because they necessarily create margins where literatures, authors, and works lie in the shadows of neglect. Even European literatures can be overlooked by all but the most narrowly focused specialists (consider Catalan, Hungarian, or modern Greek). And although the Bernheimer report recommends that "the old hostilities toward translation should be mitigated," the responses and position papers that accompanied it were divided on the issue, and translation studies continued to be peripheral in the United States.[5] Translation gained legitimacy in the British Comparative Literature Association during the 1980s, and in the following decade British universities witnessed a mushrooming of degree programs that trained translators and specialized in translation research. U.S. comparatists, in contrast, concentrated unwaveringly on original compositions by canonical writers. With rare exceptions, a scholar's decision to translate or to study translations was likely to jeopardize an academic career.

As the Bernheimer report made clear, comparatists still looked askance at translation because of their investment in "the necessity and unique benefits of a deep knowledge of foreign languages"—even though translation can't be expertly studied or practiced without such an investment.[6] At the start of the new millennium, however, the continuing marginality of translation also seemed to result from an uncertainty as to what it is and does. Haun Saussy's subsequent report for the ACLA, a collection of nineteen essays that assess "The State of the Discipline, 2004," includes an unprecedented essay on the valuable contribution that translation might make to the study of comparative literature.[7] But Saussy's own essay expresses a certain disdain for translation by implicating it in "thematic reading": "What comes across in thematic reading (a tactic devised in response to conditions of our encounter with translated literature) is not necessarily what is most worth knowing about a work."[8] The misguided reader is able to concentrate on theme, Saussy believes, because in translation "nothing of the work may survive the process but the subject matter."[9]

On this point Saussy agrees with Auerbach. Although Auerbach's ideal audience would seem to command eight languages at various stages of historical development (namely, Hebrew, ancient Greek, Latin, Italian, French, Spanish, German, and English), for his less knowledgeable readers he provides German translations of the passages he discusses. He assumes that the translations transmit the content necessary to make his readings intelligible. In effect, he treats that content as a semantic invariant on the basis of an instrumental model of translation.

Yet this assumption seems oddly credulous for comparatists with the range of languages known by Auerbach and Saussy (who was trained as both a classicist and a Sinologist). Translation can maintain a semantic correspondence, but surely this relation to the source text shouldn't be confused with giving back its theme unaltered. Translation detaches the source text from the diverse contexts that make it uniquely meaningful, valuable, and functional in the language and culture where it originated. Simultaneously, even while maintaining a semantic correspondence, translation builds a different set of contexts in the translating language, supportive of meanings, values, and functions that are new to both the source text and the receiving culture. Hence Saussy can assert that "a translator always perturbs the settled economy of two linguistic systems."[10] But then why does he also think that "a translation always brings across most successfully aspects of a work for which its audience is already prepared"?[11] Can an audience thus prepared also tolerate a translation that perturbs its language? How can a translation at once frustrate and satisfy reader expectations, particularly if it merely transmits source-text content intact? Saussy doesn't explain.

The uncertainty reflected in his essay, given its appearance in a report on the state of the field, may well be representative of comparative literature in the United States. So we shouldn't be surprised to learn that over the past decade some departments and programs have created curricular space for translation. Or that they comprise a small minority. A trawl through college and university websites indicates that approximately 25 percent of the schools currently offering comparative literature in some form include translation theory, history, and practice in their course inventories; a few have even instituted certificates. But the figure seems appallingly low for a field that could not exist without the extensive use of translations. And the situation seems not to have changed much since 2005, when a report on the undergraduate curriculum in comparative literature showed that 76.2 percent of the forty schools responding required courses on world literature in translation, but only 14.3 percent required courses in the theory and practice of translation.[12] The courses in translation, moreover, are staffed by faculty who had already nurtured an interest in translation or who were willing to retool in a new area. Not until 2011 did a department of comparative literature (at the University of Oregon) conduct a search for a tenure-track assistant professor with a specialty in translation studies. The search has so far proven to be an isolated instance.

The 2017 ACLA report presents an opportunity to gauge the extent to which translation has now entered the field. On this go-round, instead of a document produced by a committee and made the object of relatively brief responses, a "State of the Discipline" website was created to post submissions of varying lengths vetted by an editorial board, and a selection of these postings subsequently saw print in a volume edited by Ursula Heise. In the end, "over fifty texts" and "sixty participants" were involved, writing under such rubrics as "paradigms," "ideas of the decade," and "futures," and so Heise felt justified in concluding that "a rough map of our discipline's current conceptual topography emerges."[13] In this topography, translation would seem to occupy a miniscule yet still embattled space. A search on the website using the keyword "translation" yields only five postings, not all of which focus on translation. Obviously, it is not regarded as a burning issue in the field. The selection of postings gathered in the printed volume confirms that opinion remains divided as to whether texts produced by interlingual translation can serve as the basis for research and teaching, so that what Bernheimer called "the old hostilities" persist without a doubt: Saussy's chapter in the 2017 report is not alone in complaining that literature "taught predominantly in translation" leads to "lightening up the language requirements and the corresponding cultural information."[14]

When, one wonders, will comparatists realize that no necessary connection exists between teaching in translation and setting foreign language requirements? When will they admit that their research and teaching unavoidably depend on translations? And when will they therefore stop whining about an ineradicable state of affairs and instead apply their energy and expertise to learning how to read translations as texts in their own right? When, in other words, will comparatists acknowledge that translations can contribute to the understanding of the source texts they translate for the very reason that they interpret rather than reproduce those texts?

Meanwhile the three chapters in the 2017 report devoted primarily to translation don't offer much evidence of progress. On the contrary, they indicate various forms of stagnation or derailment in institutionalizing translation studies. Brigitte Rath argues that "pseudotranslation," a term applied to an original composition that is presented as a translation of a nonexistent source text, should be adopted "as a mode of reading," since it "sharpens some central concepts of comparative literature" and "opens up a new approach to literary texts."[15] Although Rath relies on the definition of the term formulated over twenty years ago by the translation scholar Gideon Toury, she never considers what it might mean for translation.

Shaden Tageldin takes up the recent insistence on "untranslatability," arguing paradoxically that any "untranslatable" language use "is at once relative and absolute, human and divine," and suggesting that comparative literature abandon "the tautology of translatability/untranslatability" for Lu Xun's "hard translation," essentially a strategy of close adherence to the source text.[16] A translation strategy might yield productive insights as part of a literary research project or pedagogy. But would not the emphasis on one such strategy ultimately skew any historical narrative or textual analysis? And why single out an early twentieth-century Chinese use of the strategy when it dates back to antiquity in various cultures, East and West?

Lucas Klein's chapter admirably recommends that translation practice be considered an interpretive act and therefore a form of scholarship, noting that "the denigration of translation relies on a privileging of the 'original' as read in the language of its composition."[17] Klein's approach is to argue by assertion, however, not through detailed cases or fresh data, and his assertions have been so often repeated as to hark back to an earlier situation that no longer obtains in the field. André Lefevere pointed out in 1982 that the concept of authorial originality denigrates translation, and in 2011 the Executive Council of the Modern Language Association of America (MLA) adopted a statement on the evaluation of translations as scholarship.[18] If these earlier documents have not substantially altered the institutional status of translation, mere reiteration seems unlikely to help. In what, we might strategically ask, does the *translator's* originality consist if it cannot be called authorial? And have the MLA guidelines ever been used to evaluate translations in peer review at an American academic institution, whether in North or South America?

Perhaps the most telling signs of how comparative literature continues to marginalize translation appear as blind spots in the 2017 report, unreflective commentary and editing that reveal a real effort to exclude translation studies from the field. In a chapter on the environmental humanities, Heise herself explains that she recently planned an essay on the many translations of Rachel Carson's *Silent Spring* (1962) so as to "highlight the importance of nonfiction prose and documentary film for environmental thought and activism," but "overcome by a sense of unease" she decided that the multiauthored report, *The Limits to Growth* (1972), was preferable because it "was mentioned most frequently"—only to reject this text as well because it could not be classified as "literary storytelling."[19]

I take the "unease" as symptomatic of institutional contradictions that Heise finds difficult to manage. To research the translations of these nonfiction texts would edge her work toward cultural rather than literary studies, the very tension that the Bernheimer report uncovered in the field, but she wound up making the conservative or backward-looking choice, regardless of the fact that translation analysis comprehends formal features like register and style, discourse and genre—features that can be considered properly "literary." Besides, isn't *The Limits to Growth* an example of "nonfiction prose"? Would Heise also decline to examine the various versions of a related text like Thomas Malthus's *An Essay on the Principle of Population* (1789), which in the century after its publication was translated into French, German, Russian, and Spanish? Ironically, she chose to develop "a more conventional argument" by discussing "environmentalist" novels that include translations from Chinese and Spanish, although she does not comment on these translations as translations, making the instrumentalist assumption that they reproduce semantic invariants in the source texts.[20] The message seems clear: translation research does not qualify as the basis of a "conventional argument" in comparative literature, and the professional unease that translation might cause is better repressed by excluding it altogether through instrumentalism.

This attitude might explain why the most exciting posting about translation on the ACLA website was not included in the printed report. Under the rubric of "practices," Daniela Kato and Bruce Allen describe their study of a medieval Japanese text that is "the product of a locally-inflected environmentalism," and that through numerous modern translations can "carry seemingly far-reaching implications within a comparative ecocritical framework."[21] Kato and Allen's incisive exposition synthesizes a broad range of materials and thereby demonstrates that their project contributes to a number of fields, including Japanese literary history, environmental literary theory and criticism, the theory of world literature, and, most uniquely, translation theory and history. This research is not only comparative, but transnational and eminently interdisciplinary, moving from the local to the global in examining the cultural and social impact of translated texts. Excluding it from *Futures of Comparative Literature* offers a truncated image of what is possible in the field, raising the question of whether an investment in these futures will yield much of a return.

On the Shoulders of World Literature

The institutional developments that affected translation over the past two decades were motivated in part by the most decisive change that comparative literature has witnessed since the influx of European theoretical discourses in the 1960s and after. Goethe's concept of "world" literature was revived, now informed by categories drawn from Bourdieu's sociology of cultural value and Immanuel Wallerstein's world-systems theory. As a result, the purview of comparative literature became international on a planetary scale. In controversial yet groundbreaking studies like Pascale Casanova's *The World Republic of Letters* (1999) and Franco Moretti's "Conjectures on World Literature" (2000),[22] global literary relations consist of a competition driven by the unequal distribution of cultural prestige and authority, on the one hand, and linguistic and literary resources, on the other. Metropolitan centers in the West (Paris, London, New York) assign value to national literary traditions as well as to specific authors and works through such practices as publishing, translation, and award-giving. Genres like the novel evolve in different literatures through the combination of foreign, usually European forms with local content.

This approach to world literature suffers from an Occidentalism, to be sure, ignoring the centers that exist in peripheries (Arabic publishing in Beirut, for instance, or translations into Indian English published in Calcutta). But it emphasizes the changing hierarchies in which literatures around the world are positioned, and it recognizes the crucial importance of transnational influence and reception, challenging the notion of autonomous national traditions. This sort of comparative thinking is far more compelling than the Anglocentric work on transnationalism coming out of English departments—Jahan Ramazani's *A Transnational Poetics* (2009), say, or Rebecca Walkowitz's *Born Translated: The Contemporary Novel in an Age of World Literature* (2015)—where the aggressive monolingualism of the U.S. academy entirely excludes foreign languages and literatures.[23] Neither Ramazani nor Walkowitz gives any serious consideration to *interlingual* translation, effectively emptying terms like "transnationalism" and "translation" of much of their significance while reaffirming the global hegemony of English.

In Walkowitz's case, this exclusion is especially fraught with inconsistency. She argues that "translation saturates our everyday culture of reading, writing, and viewing," but she discusses no translated texts, even when she quotes Kazuo Ishiguro—an author to whom she devotes substantial attention—as saying that "the rhythm of my own prose is very much like those Russian translations that I read."[24] Walkowitz's notion of contemporary novels as "born-translated" refers primarily to original compositions in English that deploy translation as theme and trope or as code-switching and shifts between dialects. The suggestion she attributes to Benedict Anderson's *Imagined Communities* (1983)—that "the repression of translation may be tied, as it is in Anderson's text, to the repression of transnational impulses within national projects"—bears an uncanny resemblance to her own project in its maintenance of a canon of Anglophone novelists taught in U.S. English departments.[25]

In the meantime the discourse on world literature among comparatists has developed unevenly, even in contradiction. David Damrosch's study, *What Is World Literature?* (2003), ranging widely over works from antiquity to the present, made an appreciable advance: the literature that deserves the label "world," Damrosch argues, is quite simply literature that crosses borders.[26] It is not a canon of works but a mode of receiving them, and translation is preeminent among the practices that perform the worlding. All the same, Damrosch's multivolume collection *The Longman Anthology of World Literature* (2004) does in fact cleave to a global canon that is immediately recognizable, packaging it chronologically for classroom use and printing every non-English work in English translation.[27] Despite this absolute dependence on translations, the pressing questions raised by teaching translated literature—Why was a particular translation chosen? What interpretation does it inscribe in the source text? How does that interpretation answer to the Anglophone cultural situation where the translation was produced?—go unformulated by the army of editors who assembled the volumes. A step in this direction was taken in the second edition (2009) with the inclusion of subsections called "Translations," short essays that comment on differences between source texts and English versions. Yet this step, even though promising, is hindered by the editors' rhetoric of loss: far from regarding translation as interpretation, the commentary assumes an instrumental model and faults the versions for failing to transfer invariant features of the source text. In "Goethe's Mignon," commenting on two translations of a song from *Wilhelm Meister's Apprenticeship*, the editor asserts that "translations are always less evocative than their originals. . . . The poetry lies in the tiniest details, the ones translators cannot but traduce."[28]

An anthology that deploys Damrosch's emphasis on border-crossing could be a fascinating experiment. It might show not only that the patterns of influence and reception constitutive of world literature are historically variable, coalescing in different canons and margins over time, but also that world literature involves diverse practices, including translation, adaptation, and editing, as well as diverse readerships, elite and popular, professional and pleasure-seeking. This anthology wouldn't be the darling of publishers: its selections can be no more than provisional, depending on how certain editors interpret literary history and which works they choose to illustrate their interpretations. Different anthologies might be edited at different moments, as global literary relations unfold through cultural exchange and as images of the past are revised in academic research.

What we call world literature would thus be constantly shifting, and its contingency might illuminate the many ways that literatures develop under the impact of transnational tendencies, whatever their location. It would also be seen as undergoing geographical redefinition according to the language through which a text crosses cultural borders. A reception-oriented anthology could pose such questions as why, in the current Anglophone canon of world literature, writers like Orhan Pamuk, Roberto Bolaño, and Yoko Tawada have displaced Italo Calvino, Gabriel García Márquez, and Assia Djebar as focuses of interest. It might even be able to explore differences in the worldwide reception of a particular contemporary writer, say, Lydia Davis or Haruki Murakami, by juxtaposing selected translations (along with annotated English versions) and sampling critical commentary. The anthology would be less a collection that affirms an existing canon than a workbook that interrogates the changing conditions of canon-formation by studying the global circulation of texts through publishing, translating, reviewing, and teaching, among other practices.

Missed Translation

Although Emily Apter nowhere mentions Damrosch's Longman anthology, she evidently has it in mind when she castigates "the entrepreneurial, bulimic drive to anthologize and curricularize the world's cultural resources, as evinced in projects sponsored by proponents of World Literature."[29] Her book, *Against World Literature* (2013), attacks what she sees as the facile form of translation driving the field of comparative literature as it enlarges its remit. Her remedy is to advocate "incommensurability," otherwise known as "the Untranslatable," so as to question "a critical praxis enabling communication across languages, cultures, time periods and disciplines."[30] This endeavor is not as perverse or nihilistic as it may at first sound in opposing "communication": it does lead Apter to gather "an array of loosely affiliated topoi," including "theologies of translation" and "the translational interdiction" as well as "literary world-systems."[31] It quickly becomes apparent, however, that "untranslatability" does not allow her to say much that is useful about translation. It is actually another way for comparative literature to repress the study of translation by assuming an instrumental model.

The problems start with Apter's reliance on French philosopher Barbara Cassin's "dictionary of untranslatables," a work of some 1,500 pages that Cassin describes (in my translation) as "a cartography of philosophical differences."[32] Published in French in 2004, it appeared in a substantially revised English version in 2014 coedited by Apter, Jacques Lezra, and Michael Wood.[33] Each entry explores a term in multiple languages, sketching its historical transmission through differences that are at once linguistic and cultural, discursive and geographical. Concepts undergo transformations that coincide with difficulties of translation. Examples—I give the English terms here—include "Subject," "Justice," "Peace," "Sex," and "World." "Each entry," Cassin remarks, "sets out from a node of untranslatability and proceeds to the comparison of terminological networks, the distortion of which comprises the history and geography of languages and cultures."[34]

Distortion? Since the terms are repeatedly mistranslated in Cassin's view, calling them "untranslatable" doesn't seem precise. In her cryptic explanation, they are "what one does not stop (not) translating."[35] Translating them is so hard as to require resourceful—and, for translators, rather routine—strategies like coining a neologism or assigning a new meaning to an old word. Instead of demonstrating untranslatability, then, the entries actually document a succession of forceful translations, so that the terms reveal an eminent *translatability*, usually stretching from Greek antiquity deep into European modernity. In Cassin's dictionary, however, some translations are permitted while others are not, and the impermissible are branded mistranslations. In poring over the entries, you soon feel that the very nature of translation is in doubt, that different contributors assume different but unstated notions of what translation is, and that even the entry on the term "To Translate [*Traduire*]" doesn't help to sort out the muddle.

Consider the entry on "Subject," authored by Cassin, Étienne Balibar, and Alain de Libera and translated into English by David Macey. Apter, treating it as typical of Cassin's project, presents an extended quotation. Here is a key part:

> One of the most famous statements, in which Averroës appears to introduce the notion of the subject, is the passage on eternity and the corruptibility of the theoretical intellect—the ultimate human perfection. It asserts: "Perhaps philosophy always exists in the greater part of the subject, just as the man exists thanks to man, and just as the horse exists thanks to horse." What does the expression mean? Going against the very principles of Averroës's noetics, the Averroist Jean de Jandun understands it to mean that "philosophy is perfect in the greater part of its subject (*sui subjecti*)," or in other words "in most men" (*in majori parte hominum*). There are no grounds for this interpretation. We can explain it, however, if we recall that Averroës's Latin translator has confused the Arabic terms *mawdu* [word in Arabic in original] (subject or substratum in the sense of *hupokeimenon*) and *mawdi* [word in Arabic in original] (place). When Averroës simply says that philosophy has always existed "in the greater part of the place," meaning "almost everywhere," Jean understands him as saying that it has as its subject "the majority of men," as every man (or almost every man) contributes to a full (perfect) realization in keeping with his knowledge and aptitudes.[36]

Any idea that Averroës's statement addresses human subjectivity is wrong, the consequence of an error made by the Latin translator of his Arabic commentary on Aristotle's Greek text, *De Anima*. And the mistranslation later misleads the fourteenth-century French thinker, Jean de Jandun, even though he is recognized as an "Averroist." Apter uncritically accepts this account, repeating its rhetoric of translation loss and agreeing with the French authors' conclusion that the mistranslation, as she puts it, "haunts modern concepts of free will, egoic autonomy, and transcendental subjecthood."[37] Nevertheless, the translation analysis raises more questions than it answers, ultimately showing that untranslatability lays a shaky foundation for an approach to the history of philosophy, let alone world literature.

Analyzing a translation requires first that a source text be established. This step may seem a simple matter of locating the text used by the translator. But editing is hardly an innocent or transparent procedure, especially with an archaic text that has undergone a complicated transmission. The authors seem aware of this problem, admitting "that Averroës's *Long Commentary on the De Anima* is, given the current state of the corpus, fully accessible only in Latin, or in Michael Scot's tricky translation (the Arabic original having been lost)."[38] Yet, if this is the case, on what basis can they quote Averroës's Arabic to identify the Latin mistranslation? Instead of quoting an extant source, they have *invented* it through a back translation. Their authority, in other words, seems to be merely their own Arabic translation from an unspecified Latin text—buttressed by their interpretation of the Andalusian philosopher's "noetics," his conception of the human intellect. To identify an error in a translation, the source text and its contents must be fixed so as to exhibit a departure, and that fixing is an interpretive act, here speculation based on the authors' understanding of Averroës's philosophy.

A second factor needed to analyze a translation is a concept of equivalence, a relation between the translation and the source text that functions as the criterion of correctness. This relation usually specifies a textual unit or division on which the translator's work focuses. The unit of translation might be the individual word, but it can just as well be the sentence, the paragraph, the chapter, even the entire text. Taking any of these divisions as the unit of translation would affect how the translator renders specific words and phrases. Cassin and her contributors, just by choosing the genre of a dictionary, take the word as their unit and assume that the translator must maintain a word-by-word correspondence in meaning between the translation and the source text. Yet because a unit is a *formal* division of a text, any unit would allow a translator to maintain some kind of semantic correspondence, whether the meaning is exact or paraphrastic, explicit or equivocal. A translator of poetry, for example, might take the poetic line as the unit of translation, selecting words so that the syllables create a certain meter or rhythm, a sound effect that might accompany the communication of meaning. Ezra Pound called this practice translating the "cantabile" or song-like values of a poem.[39]

What concept of equivalence did Averroës's Latin translator apply? Given the lack of the Arabic source, this question can't be answered with any certainty. The French authors' discovery of only one error suggests that, in their view, the translator had more than a passing acquaintance with Arabic and sought to maintain a semantic correspondence throughout. Could what seems to be an error really be a deliberate choice, reflecting a unit of translation that goes beyond the word? Medieval practices constructed various relations between the translation and the source text, some of which were much more freely inventive than the strict word-by-word equivalence that prevails today. Sandra Laugier makes precisely this point in her entry on "To Translate," noting that to consider medieval practices from a modern perspective would be "misleading."[40]

A third factor for translation analysis is the introduction of a code or theme that enables the assessment of the translation as an interpretation. Fixing the source text, applying a concept of equivalence, introducing a code—these steps are usually taken all at once during the analysis, determining accuracy, imprecision, or downright error on the translator's part. The French authors' code is their own interpretation of Averroës's noetics, the conception of the intellect they use to criticize both the Latin translation and Jean de Jandun's understanding of the philosopher's thought. But behind that code lies another, a basically poststructuralist or posthumanist discourse that inevitably highlights opposing concepts, like the autonomous, transcendental subject—and pegs them as errors. Once again, as with their modern concept of equivalence, the authors seem to have made an anachronistic move: they have imposed on medieval texts a bête noire of contemporary French philosophy.

Any charge of mistranslation conceals the various steps in a translation analysis because it assumes an instrumental model of translation. Here *to translate* means to reproduce a semantic invariant, an essential, unchanging meaning which is believed to be inherent in Averroës's Arabic text, but which both the Latin translator and Jean de Jandun failed to reproduce. Yet Jean was a distinguished master in the arts faculty at the University of Paris. He formulated a noetics that was at once Aristotelian and Averroist, eliciting criticism from Thomas Aquinas much as Averroës's own philosophy did. Intellectual historians regard Jean as giving an Augustinian cast to the Aristotelian tradition, particularly through his readings of Averroës's commentaries.[41] Jean, like the Latin translator before him, offered a bona fide interpretation, inscribing in Averroës a distinctly Christian concept of individual subjectivity. But this interpretive possibility is reduced to verbal error by the instrumentalism that underpins the entry in Cassin's dictionary.

As an understanding of translation, instrumentalism is conceptually impoverished. On the one hand, it removes a translated text from the cultural situation and historical moment that invest it with significance as an interpretive act. On the other hand, it installs the translated text in a timeless, universal realm where judgments of correctness or error are summoned to advance, through an analytical sleight of hand, a competing interpretation. As these points suggest, my discourse assumes the critique of the autonomous, transcendental subject in Continental philosophy. But to smuggle that critique into the analysis of a medieval translation without registering any historical difference is to turn the past into a mirror of the analyst's own intellectual obsessions. This form of cultural narcissism we can do without.

Made in USA

The English version of Cassin's dictionary exacerbates rather than remedies its problems. The editors have commissioned some twenty new pieces, distributed as freestanding entries or inserted as boxes in the entries translated from the French text. Most of the additions don't give much attention to translation issues; some none at all. When they are taken up, the instrumental model of translation comes into play, bringing about confusion.

Anthony Vidler devotes most of his entry on "Chôra" (variously defined as "land," "place," "space," or "room") to a carefully detailed interpretation of its "special significance" and "corresponding ambiguity" in Plato's *Timaeus*.[42] Vidler relies solely on Francis Cornford's 1937 translation with commentary, although no consideration is given to how Cornford's particular style of translation might have inflected Vidler's account. Instead he asserts that "in subsequent rereadings and reinterpretations, the Platonic *chôra* was subjected to oversimplification (Aristotle) and overinterpretation (Chrysippus, Proclus)."[43] With this assertion, Vidler effectively sets up his own Cornford-based interpretation as right while tossing later Greek philosophy into the garbage can of error. The entry then summarizes Jacques Derrida's remarks on the term and the difficulty it poses to translation, concluding that "there is, therefore, no question of proposing 'le mot juste' for *chôra*; rather than reducing it falsely to a name or essence, it has to be understood as a structure."[44] Yet it is only by reducing the term to an essential meaning, unchanging since Plato, that Vidler can determine which interpretations or translations qualify as "oversimplification" and "overinterpretation."

Occasionally, an Anglophone contributor seems much bolder than his French colleagues in impugning a translation. Ben Kafka's entry on "Media/Medium (of Communication)" juxtaposes two different versions of a passage from Freud where "words [Worte]" are called a "Vermittler" (variously translated as "mediator," "intermediary," and "broker"). Kafka rejects Jean Laplanche's French rendering, "les instruments," while strongly preferring James Strachey's, "media." Why? "Because," Kafka quips, "it works so well, perhaps better than the original."[45] Sure enough, once he starts to justify his choice, his judgment depends less on "the original" than on the question of which "term makes it easier to understand Freud's claim"—according to Kafka's interpretation of that claim, of course.[46] Between the German source text and the English translation, a third category has intervened, Kafka's own understanding of the German, and it is on that basis that a particular translation is preferred. Even at the cost of besmirching the source text. An accomplished psychoanalytic theorist like Laplanche could no doubt have justified his rendering of "Vermittler" according to his own interpretation of Freud. To adjudicate between renderings in two different languages, shouldn't we consider where and when they were devised? Or does Kafka's investment in the global lingua franca, in English, preempt a more thoughtful treatment of a French translation?

Interestingly, the polylingual context enhanced by the translation of Cassin's dictionary exposes limitations in both sets of contributions, French as well as English. Alain Pons's entry on

"Sprezzatura," the neologism that the Italian count Baldassare Castiglione coined in 1528 for the courtier's peculiar gracefulness, considers only French translations. Readers familiar with European Renaissance literatures, however, will note that Pons missed an enlightening case by ignoring Sir Thomas Hoby's 1561 English version, "recklessness," with its implicit condemnation of courtly behavior.[47] By the same token, Susan Wolfson's note on "Fancy" as distinguished from "imagination" cites only English Romantic authors, stripping the terms of their genealogy in German philosophical traditions. Although she mentions how Samuel Taylor Coleridge construed them, a reader under the spell of Wolfson's period specialization doesn't receive the slightest indication that Coleridge linked his thinking to a line stretching from Johannes Nikolaus Tetens to Kant to Fichte.[48] The very languages in which the contributors write seem to have curbed their expositions.

The most remarkable aspect of Cassin's dictionary in English is the editors' effort to assimilate the French text to the current critical orthodoxy in comparative literature as it is institutionalized in the United States, the configuration of European philosophical discourses that gave rise most notably to poststructuralism, postcolonial theory, and queer theory. Apter's preface is explicit on this point: "we felt compelled to plug specific gaps, especially those pertaining to 'theory,' understood in the Anglophone academic sense of that term."[49] Hence several well-known theorists were enlisted to provide summaries of their own work, including Judith Butler on "Gender and Gender Trouble," Gayatri Chakravorty Spivak on "Planetarity," and Robert J. C. Young on "*Colonia* and *Imperium*." Other theorists who have achieved prominence in the United States, notably Walter Benjamin, Giorgio Agamben, and Alain Badiou, play bigger parts in the English version than in the French source. This Anglocentric spin produces curiosities like the box on

"Postcolonial, Postcolonialism," written by Émilienne Baneth-Nouailhetas, the attaché for university cooperation at the French embassy in Washington DC, who cites only Anglophone theorists. Who is colonizing whom here, you might wonder? The English version so domesticates Cassin's project as to raise the question of whether the result is more academic navel-gazing. This encounter with the foreign does not put domestic institutions to the test: it enshrines rather than interrogates the theoretical and critical discourses that currently dominate the study of literature in the U.S. academy.

What happens when Cassin's dictionary is transplanted from an academic to a popular venue? Is it merely popularized for mass consumption? The questions are prompted by articles about the book in such venues as *Publishers Weekly*, *The Huffington Post*, and *World Literature Today*.[50] Written by coeditor Michael Wood, evidently to support the publication of the English version, these pieces must be considered much more than a promotion strategy or even applications that elaborate on specific entries. Insofar as the magazines have a combined readership that reaches into the millions, any exposition of Cassin's ideas can work to shape commonly held conceptions of what translation is. Of course any project that generates a conversation about translation might be welcomed in Anglophone cultures, where so little gets translated (between 2 and 4 percent of total annual book output) and what does is little noticed.[51] Yet if Cassin's dictionary were to become the main source of the talking points, the marginal status of translation would persist, unaffected, and may actually worsen.

This impression is borne out by Wood's piece on "Translating Rilke." It opens with the assertion that "No literary work corresponds more closely than Rilke's to the definition Barbara Cassin offers of the untranslatable."[52] For Wood, Rilke's writing qualifies as an untranslatable because it has been constantly retranslated into English. Beginning in the 1930s, the number of selections, complete works, and anthology compilations has grown so quickly that they now exceed one hundred books, making Rilke the most translated modern poet into English.[53]

As Wood tries to account for this compulsion to retranslate, he offers a caution: "Let's not reach for the ineffable, the notion of something mystically secreted in Rilke's language and not available anywhere else."[54] And he commendably grounds his discussion on actual translations, although what he finds, after examining multiple versions of the same lines from the first *Duino Elegy*, is admittedly not a great deal: "everyone," he remarks, "respects the word order," and "everyone translates *Dasein* as 'existence'."[55] He finds, in other words, that despite their enormous number, the retranslations don't reveal much variation in strategy or even in lexicon and syntax. He takes this fact as evidence of untranslatability, but in doing so he ignores his earlier caution and reaches for the ineffable: "we begin to sense something of the genuine disappointments of translation, our reasons for keeping on, for searching not for a final or better version but something else, something closer to a sharing of what can't be shared."[56]

"What can't be shared"? In a translation? That phrase turns Rilke's German text precisely into a mystical secret. Why does Wood's account devolve into contradiction instead of becoming more incisive and illuminating? Why doesn't he frankly state what is too obvious, that the retranslations haven't justified their existence, that their minimal variation points to weak, entropic interpretations that put into question whether Anglophones need yet another and another and another version?

This admission would require Wood to look elsewhere, away from Rilke's poetry—which clearly cannot in itself explain the repeated retranslations—and toward the translating culture, where literary traditions and values always inform the choice of texts for translation. Rilke's poetry has proven to be so irresistible to Anglophone literary taste, one argument might run, because British and North American poetries from the beginning of the twentieth century have been dominated by a belated romanticism that bears some resemblance to Rilke's forms and themes, right down to the idea that poetry should be evocative of the ineffable. In a letter from 1923, for instance, Rilke explains that his writing aims "to correct wherever possible the old repressions which have taken from us our secrets," including the "formidableness" of "life itself": "Anyone who has not acknowledged the fearsomeness of life on occasion, even acclaimed it, will never fully take possession of the ineffable authorities of our existence."[57]

In following Cassin, however, Wood stresses only the relation that translation constructs to the source text, neglecting the relation to the translating culture that ultimately takes priority. Glimpses of the latter relation appear in his recurrent expressions of dissatisfaction with the translations: "Shouldn't we be looking for something more inventive here?"; "Instances of similar difficulties and shortfalls arise with translations of the end of the fourth *Duino Elegy*"; "We all have 'understand' for *einsehen*, but why can't we do better?"; "The last attempt seems just wrong."[58] But such expressions imply the application of a criterion of judgment that remains unstated, whether some notion of a good poem or an interpretation of the German text that is assumed to be inherent in it (possibly both). Thus Wood's discourse displays the instrumentalism of Cassin's project, a formal or semantic invariant is hinted at but never articulated (the ineffable again), and the reader who seeks to be enlightened about the English Rilke winds up getting only Wood's personal preferences: "It does, to my ear, feel less contorted"; "Even the word *stehn* has for me a curious ambiguity"; "I have a fondness for 'farewell' in this context."[59] The notion of untranslatability defangs Wood's examination of the retranslations, locking it into a rather old-fashioned comparison between the translated and source texts and preempting a more self-conscious analysis that would avoid mere self-regard.

Untranslatability as Word-Surfing

Cassin's dictionary, whether in French or in English, is an astonishingly rich compendium of European philosophical traditions. But readers should treat her notion of untranslatability with suspicion. Apter's *Against World Literature* elevates it to a methodological principle, unfortunately, and the results seem misguided. Relying on Cassin's dictionary not only straightjackets Apter's interpretations in a peculiarly French philosophical discourse; it also risks turning back the clock in comparative literature, returning to the Eurocentrism that characterized the field in the past. Except for Arabic and Hebrew, only European languages contain untranslatables for Cassin and her contributors. (The English version hushes up this aspect of Cassin's project by deleting the word *européen* from her title.) When Apter gets down to particular cases, furthermore, she translates with such glib facility that her criticism of the proponents of world literature applies to her own work—in spades.

Her chapter on two Portuguese words she designates as untranslatables, *fado* and *saudade*, is typical. It opens with translations of them, the former as "melancholia, pleasure, ecstasy," the latter as "nostalgia, moral ambiguity."[60] But since untranslatability for Apter means not the inability to translate but repeated, relentless translation, she gives the English parenthetically and without comment, as if it didn't matter. Then the translations that interest her begin, as she rapidly segues between disparate texts where *saudade* is said to figure as a "keyword" (*fado* disappears). They include novels by the contemporary Portuguese writer António Lobo Antunes, the entry on the Portuguese language in Cassin's dictionary, Rimbaud's "The Drunken Boat," Flaubert's *Madame Bovary*, the Italian novelist Antonio Tabucchi's *Requiem: A Hallucination*, Orhan Pamuk's *Istanbul*, Fernando Pessoa's *Book of Disquiet*, and finally the French philosopher Quentin Meillassoux's concept of "transfinitude," which becomes the ultimate meaning of the Portuguese untranslatable. An interpretation that had initially seemed local, relating the words to Portuguese history and politics through Lobo Antunes's novels, then expansive by incorporating a wider range of reference turns out to be utterly reductive: Apter removes texts from their traditions, situations, and moments, quotes them in English translations without commenting on those translations (except for Samuel Beckett's Rimbaud, said to be "alive to the *saudade-effect*"), and ends up equating everything to a single concept.[61] Apter occasionally inserts self-conscious qualifications—"Saudade here risks becoming overly capacious" or "Such a translation, monstrous though it may be"—but these comments never betray the slightest awareness that the literature is being read so superficially.[62]

Chapter after chapter shows that Apter's exposition intensifies the questionable effects of the instrumentalism she inherits from Cassin's dictionary. Apter defines the untranslatable as "an incorruptible or intransigent nub of meaning that triggers endless translating in response to its singularity."[63] Yet if meaning is "incorruptible or intransigent," we are dealing with an invariant, not a variable interpretation, and she has articulated a semantic essentialism leading to judgments of mistranslation that favor her own interpretation. Hence she describes her task as "gauging the deformations, reformulations, and temporal *décalages* of translated works."[64] This description boils down to a centuries-old idea of translation: it defines and privileges the source text through a romantic concept of original integrity—the means of measuring the "deformations"—and thereby disparages translations as the destruction or contamination of that integrity, treating them as perpetual yet insufficient compromises. Whenever the notion of "compromise" is used to describe translation, instrumentalism is at work: it assumes the existence of a source-text invariant that a translation can approximate but never reproduce, in Apter's case a notion of "singularity."

It is one thing to recognize that translating constantly confronts incommensurability but another, very different thing to call the resulting translation a "deformation." Translating operates by building an interpretive context in a language and culture that differ from those that constitute the source text. When translated, therefore, the source text becomes the site of multiple and conflicting interpretations—even when the translator consults a dictionary on every word (indeed, dictionaries can proliferate the possibilities). Witness the history of Bible translation or the retranslations of the great modernist writers, Franz Kafka and Marcel Proust, Thomas Mann and Italo Svevo. To erect one interpretation over others requires a justification that amounts to another interpretive act, the cogency of which, as with every interpretation, is contingent on the institutional conditions under which it is performed. It is these conditions that trigger translations, never the source text itself or its "singularity." Academic institutions in particular house procedures of reading and conventions of documentation that permit certain interpretations to the exclusion of others, preferring translations that maintain the status quo and marginalizing those that contest it—unless, of course, they foster the emergence of a new consensus. Because Apter's notion of untranslatability is essentialist, it cannot enable an account of the contingencies of translation. Not surprisingly, she considers only one translated text with any sustained attention: Eleanor Marx Aveling's English version of *Madame Bovary* (1886). The analysis, however, is less than convincing.

Taking the same unit of translation as Cassin's dictionary, Apter discusses only a few words in Marx's version (although, strangely, none is called an untranslatable). She praises Marx's choice of "wealth" instead of "riches" to render Flaubert's use of "la richesse" because "wealth" reflects the ideas of her father Karl, "as if Eleanor Marx were intent on not letting Anglophone readers forget that luxury items . . . were dressed-up versions of money, hardened into congealed capital."[65] True, "wealth" appeared in Adam Smith's famous treatise, which Karl Marx sought to challenge, but if the word denoted some theoretically specific economic or political meaning in the late nineteenth century, it isn't documented in the *Oxford English Dictionary*, where "wealth" and "riches" are synonymous. Raymond Williams's *Keywords* (1976) includes a useful entry on "wealth" in which he observes that "the modern sense is clear enough" in the fourteenth century when wealth was said "To make us riche for evermore."[66] Even if "wealth" did carry the suggestion of a Marxist critique, would the translator have plausibly assigned it to Emma Bovary, whose point of view seems to govern the passage where it is used, the description of the Vaubyessard ball? No, "riches," if it is indeed less conceptually sophisticated, even somewhat poetical, would better suit Emma's ingenuous romanticism. If the translator had rendered "la richesse" as "capital," the translation might justifiably be called Marxist. But Apter doesn't think through these issues. And she presents no evidence for construing "wealth" as she does.

To make sense of Eleanor Marx's translation, more than one word obviously needs to be considered. Much can be learned about her particular interpretation by examining her treatment of important episodes in the narrative, analyzing how her verbal choices nuance point of view and characterization. On the basis of such passages, we can infer not only the concept of equivalence she applied in her translating, but also the values, beliefs, and social representations that may have guided her shaping of the characters and their actions. These factors of the translator's interpretation—*interpretants*, I prefer to call them, both formal and thematic—can be articulated only against the analyst's interpretation of the French text, which then becomes the means of indicating points of conformity and divergence. More can be learned by situating Marx's strategies in relation to Victorian practices of translating prose fiction. The aim is not to consider her translation as an original composition, but to analyze it as a text in its own right, intervening into a particular cultural situation at a particular historical moment and for that reason relatively autonomous from the source text it translates. To historicize a translation at once distinguishes it from the present and allows its differences to mark the limitations of the analyst's time-bound interpretation and method. It is only this sort of analysis that can provide compelling evidence for the social significance of Marx's work, the ideological determinations that Apter wants to locate in it.

Apter argues that Marx's brief prefatory comment on her translation, as well as her practice, "affords a glimpse of a language of labor released from a transcendental, capitalist logic of equivalence, exchange, project and credit."[67] She quotes most of Marx's comment, assuming that the translator's self-characterization as a "conscientious worker" is sufficient to support her reading. But Marx was a professional translator, politically committed yet nonetheless dependent on translation for her livelihood.[68] Given the generally low rates paid to translators in her period, her labor on even a notorious novel like *Madame Bovary* was likely to have earned her much less than her publisher's return on his investment. We don't know what Marx got paid in 1886, but Russian translator Constance Garnett received £40 for her 283 page version of Goncharov's *A Common Story* in 1894, when an unfurnished London flat might cost a middle-class working woman an annual rent that ranged between £24 (for two rooms) and £69 (for four).[69] The fact that humanistic translation still doesn't pay a subsistence wage in Anglophone cultures makes Apter's call for translators to "deoown" their work not an "activist" strategy but sheer capitulation to exploitive copyright codes and publishing contracts.[70]

Worse, Apter's quotation of Marx's comment is incomplete. After Marx describes her translation as "faithful," stating that she "neither suppressed nor added a line, a word," Apter omits a passage that displays Marx's obsession with equivalence:

> That often I have not found the best possible word to express Flaubert's meaning I know; but those who have studied him will understand how impossible it must be for any one to give an exact reproduction of the inimitable style of the master. He spent "days seeking one word." The consequence is that he invariably gives one word that fully expresses his meaning. We may search through all Littré and find none other so appropriate; and yet, while feeling its absolute fitness, we may not be able to give its exact equivalent in another tongue.[71]

Eleanor Marx assumed an instrumental model of translation: the author's intended meaning is "fully" expressed in his text, and the translator's job is to reproduce it. Yet this model, along with her idolization of "the master," could only dampen the spark of inventiveness necessary to emulate Flaubert's style. Far from breaking with capitalist logic, her preface and her practice are inextricably caught within it, whether materially in her own exploited wage labor or metaphorically in the equivalent form she worked to produce in her translation, the economy of one word exchanged for one word. By linking the impossibility of translating Flaubert to "those who have studied him," Marx unwittingly belies her instrumentalism: her remark shows that translation is hermeneutic, dependent on commentary articulated independently even as it inscribes its own interpretations.

Theory vs. Practice?

Apter has simply asserted her reading of Marx's translation, not argued it with textual analyses and historical research. It is purely speculative, lacking any grounding in empirical data, making only the rare textual reference. It is the epitome of theoreticism, a fetishizing of theoretical concepts at the expense of linguistic, cultural, and social specificity. For the fact is that Apter is interested only in theory, not in translation. After dismissing centuries of "philosophy in translation studies" because it refers to "professional practice," she announces that "what interests me most is something more pointed: what does it mean to think of translation as a kind of philosophy, or as a way of doing theory and its history?"[72]

Yet the priority Apter gives to theory is retrograde. It signals her nostalgia for the moment of High Theory in the humanities during the 1980s, such that the only "philosophies of translation" she recognizes are those "developed by Jacques Derrida, Gayatri Chakravorty Spivak, Samuel Weber, Barbara Johnson, Abdel-fattah Kilito and Édouard Glissant," in addition to Cassin.[73] Apter's unexamined investment in these "philosophies" leads her to draw the naïve distinction between theory and practice that appears in the remarks of so many translators as well as the many academics who must use translations in their research and teaching, all of them unaware that no verbal choices can be made in translating except on the basis of theoretical assumptions. A translation of a travel guidebook or a restaurant menu can therefore be a way of doing theory too, although it lacks the cachet of the theoretical discourses to which Apter subscribes.

Her allegiance, however, is inconsistent. She has apparently forgotten Derrida's paradox—"In a sense, nothing is untranslatable; but *in another sense* everything is untranslatable"—although instrumentalism, as we shall see in the next chapter, exerts an insidious hold on Derrida's thinking as well.[74]

Apter's reliance on the current critical orthodoxy leads to half-baked formulations that require more careful exposition to make sense, but that would still seem of dubious value in understanding translation. Take her cursory reference to Samuel Weber's examination of Walter Benjamin's "-abilities," the German thinker's habit of constructing concepts by nominalizing verbs with the suffix *-barkeit*, as in "translatability" (*Übersetzbarkeit*), so as to signify "potentiality" as opposed to "*actuality* as mere facts."[75] Apter wants to coin the term "*unübersetz-barkeit* to refer to that which impedes translational fluency yet enables critical faculties nonetheless."[76]

Yet is this coinage intended to suggest that untranslatables exist only potentially, not actually? Wouldn't a potential untranslatability be inconsequential (or nonsensical) for both the theory and practice of translation? The word "impedes" would seem to imply the actual existence of an untranslatable, thus undercutting the reference to Weber's study. Besides, what exactly does "translational fluency" mean? Does it indicate a too facile or slapdash movement from the source to the translated text, perhaps translating that is too assimilative to receiving cultural values? Or does it indicate a translated text that is easily readable and therefore immediately accessible, so that the retention of a word from the source text (would that be an untranslatable or just untranslated?) might affect readability? Or does "translational fluency" carry both of these possible senses? Regardless, couldn't a detailed context sufficiently saturate an untranslated word with meaning to effect a translation? How, moreover, are "critical faculties" enabled by the simple retention of a source-language word? Doesn't the reader need to bring to the reading experience a set of concepts and procedures to make that word yield a particular significance, interpreting it or effectively translating it into a critical discourse? Apter doesn't bother to answer such questions. She privileges theory to such an extent that she evidently expects the mere citation of Weber's densely speculative discussion, as well as its relation to her project, to be intelligible without explanation. As a result, not only does Apter never make her point clear, but the materiality of translation is evaporated into abstraction.

This problem should not come as a surprise, in the end, since it also occurs in Weber's study of Benjamin, although here it appears as omissions and inconsistencies in his argument. In treating Benjamin's "-ability" suffix as a means of philosophizing, Weber understands the concept of "translatability" as emphasizing linguistic form over meaning, "a *way*—a way of signifying—rather than a *what*," whereby "a determining function" is assigned to "*syntax* over *semantics*," and "literal" or "interlinear" translation, adhering closely to the syntactical features of the source text, becomes the strategy that materializes the diverse ways of signifying that are constitutive of "pure language," or "the movement of symbolization itself."[77] Yet previous commentators on Benjamin's "pure language" are in fact divided about its significance, disclosing an indeterminacy in his treatment of the concept: it has been taken as designating either "a return to the Adamic unison of human speech," in the sense of "a utopian moment in which all speech is immediate to meaning," or "a Babelian event," in the sense of "the being-language of language, tongue or language *as such*, that unity without any self-identity, which makes for the fact that there are languages and that they are languages."[78] On the one hand, "pure language" is Kabbalistic mysticism; on the other, it is tantamount to Derridean deconstruction. Weber suppresses this indeterminacy while siding with the second reading, construing translatability as "a relational dynamic that is precisely not self-identical but perpetually in the process of alteration, transformation, becoming-other."[79] Once again, however, the materiality of the translated text risks vanishing amid philosophical abstraction. To prevent that, I want to raise a much more practical question: in Weber's account, what happens to meaning in translation?

He himself brings up the issue. The notion that "translation simply ignores the meaning of the original," according to Weber, "would be hard to imagine," and so he explains that the literal translation "involves the interplay of the different *possible* meanings of the original text and of the translation," resulting "not in a single meaning but rather in a *difference of meanings*."[80] This semantic proliferation reveals that the concepts Benjamin constructs through the "-ability" suffix "refer to what Jacques Derrida, writing in *Limited Inc.* (1988) of his quasi-concept, 'iterability,' called 'structural possibilities,' the necessity of which does not depend on actual fact or probable implementation."[81]

But if translatability is a case of iterability, then *any* translation, not only a literal translation, would release or enact that feature of language. And insofar as translation recontextualizes the source text in a different language and culture, it changes *both* the form and meaning of that text, altering whatever significance it bore in its originary language and culture. Derrida in fact illustrates iterability with a translation. The expression, "the green is or" (*oder*), used by Edmund Husserl as an example of agrammaticality in the "oriented contextual field" constructed by the *Logical Investigations* (1900–1901)—which includes the German language—acquires grammaticality when it is translated into French: "Where has the green (of the grass) gone (*le vert est où*)?"[82] Since, as Derrida observes, a signifying chain "can break with every given context and engender infinitely new con-texts in an absolutely nonsaturable fashion," a text can support many different interpretations and many different translations.[83] Does Weber really have this point in mind when he refers to translatability as "structural possibilities" or "a difference of meanings"? If so, why does he repeatedly fault Harry Zohn's translation of Benjamin's essay, "The Task of the Translator"? Shouldn't Weber acknowledge that because of iterability the German text can support "different *possible* meanings"?

As Weber begins his exposition of translatability, however, he judges Zohn's translation to be inadequate:

> First, "translatability" is defined as a function of the "nexus of life" (*Zusammenhang des Lebens*). Second, this nexus is described in terms not of "life" as such, but rather as what Benjamin calls the living (*das Lebendige*). This, of course, tends to get effaced in the translation (although it could easily enough have been preserved): "Just as the utterances [*Äußerungen*] of life are most intimately tied to the living [not to "the phenomenon of life"—sw], without signifying anything for it, so translation issues from the original. Not so much from its life as from its 'after-life'" (GS4, 10; SW1, 254). What characterizes Benjamin's language, in German, and what once again tends to get lost in the English transla-tion, is the critical movement of departure, of taking-leave, a movement that moves outward and away. The word that is translated in the published version simply as "phenom-ena" is in fact literally constructed around the prefix "out-" (*aus*) and the adjective or adverb *außer*, meaning "outside of," "except."[84]

Weber continues to criticize Zohn's translation, but enough has been quoted to make clear that what "tends to get effaced" or "lost" in that version is not, strictly speaking, Benjamin's meaning but rather Weber's *interpretation* of that meaning. Zohn does maintain a semantic correspondence to the German; he just applies a different concept of equivalence, less "literally" focused on the word and its syntactical features, and he inscribes a different interpretation, one that might be worth studying on its own terms (does his insertion of the word "phenomenon," for instance, reflect a Kantian discourse?), but that obviously does not agree with Weber's.

For the fact is that their interpretations could not possibly agree. Zohn, a Viennese émigré who earned a Harvard doctorate in German and joined the German faculty of Brandeis University in 1951, was translating Benjamin in the mid-1960s, whereas Weber's approach, as Carlo Salzani has remarked, is "to look for *correspondances* with contemporary practices of interpretation," academic trends such as deconstruction, so that Weber applies "a pre-established 'theory,' a discourse and a language external to it [Benjamin's work], in order to co-opt him as a predecessor."[85] When Weber criticizes Zohn's translation for not having "preserved" Benjamin's meaning, he jettisons the concept of iterability and makes the instrumentalist assumption that his particular interpretation, as well as the translation that inscribes it, reproduce the semantic invariant contained in the German text. Weber needs to fix a meaning in order to assert that Zohn's translation departs from it, but he doesn't regard that fixing as provisional, even though it foregrounds a meaning that, according to Weber's Derridean approach, can be no more than one possibility among a profusion of others. Zohn's version of Benjamin's essay in effect challenges Weber's interpretation, forcing him to disclose his instrumental model of translation, although without any critical self-awareness that would qualify his transformation of the German text into a reflection of his own intellectual interests. Instead Weber responds to that challenge by dismissing Zohn's version under the guise of correction.

Political Action Kneecapped

Perhaps the most lamentable consequence of Apter's book is to feed the malaise that has recently beset left-wing thinking. Although she claims to offer a theory of translation that represents a conceptual and political advance over the theories circulating in comparative literature and translation studies, she sheds no light on the kind of translating that occurs routinely, whether in the publishing industry, in academic institutions, among diasporic communities and exiles, or in diplomacy, occupied territories, and military conflict. She devotes an entire chapter to the argument that the use of "border-crossing" as a metaphor for translation ignores the "checkpoint" where sovereignty and occupation are enforced.[86] Fair enough. But she considers only projects by artists, architects, and writers, and untranslatability becomes a metaphor for getting stopped at the border. No effort is made to engage with the now substantial body of research on translation in asylum hearings and wartime, books like Robert Barsky's *Constructing a Productive Other* (1994) and Moira Inghilleri's *Interpreting Justice* (2012) as well as Vicente Rafael's articles on interpreters in the Iraq war.[87]

Here untranslatability is not an aesthetic or philosophical category but a set of lived relations to opposed constituencies, provoking suspicion, insult, and violence. During the U.S. occupation of Iraq, Rafael points out, Iraqi nationals who served as Arabic interpreters for the American military were "targeted by insurgents and reviled by most Iraqis," while for the soldiers the interpreters' "indispensability [was] also the source of their duplicity, making them seem to be potential insurgents."[88] This predicament puts the lie to "the American notion of translation as monolingual assimilation with its promise of democratic communication and the just exchange of meanings."[89] But it also leads to alienation, destruction, and death. Rafael deploys a notion of untranslatability that resembles Apter's: translation "consists in the proliferation and confusion of possible meanings and therefore in the impossibility of arriving at a single one."[90] We come away from Rafael's account, however, with a renewed sense of the importance of translation in realizing utopian aspirations for social life: we can choose to question and avoid any assimilative notion of translation by studying and practicing it as an interpretive act that seeks to register the linguistic and cultural differences of source texts and cultures while interrogating receiving cultural situations.

Apter discourages any academic who wishes to investigate the politics of translation by smearing translation as dubious. To be sure, translation plays a significant role in driving the current geopolitical economy. The forms and practices that are translated worldwide include contracts and patents, instruction manuals and software packages, advertisements and brand names, film and video soundtracks, bestsellers and children's literature, political speeches and public service information, and journalism in various formats, print, electronic, and digital. Nonetheless, translation can be turned into a site of ideological critique and political resistance, directed not only against multinational corporations, financial institutions, and government agencies but also against ideological ensembles like cultural stereotypes—although the extent and success of such interventions depend crucially on educating the many agents involved in the production, circulation, and reception of translations.[91] Hence to promote a notion of untranslatability so as to stigmatize and rule out the study of translation in its many forms, humanistic, pragmatic, and technical, as well as the institutional and economic conditions in which it is practiced—any such exclusion is effectively to abdicate to the status quo by withdrawing from the areas where social struggles can occur. What ideological force can a notion of untranslatability possess in the absence of political engagement through the selection of source texts and the development of discursive strategies to translate them, through the strategic choice of social forms and practices as points of intervention, and through an accompanying pedagogical initiative to support the understanding and use of translations? Since Apter neither considers nor offers such proposals, restricting her commentary to theoretical speculation, the notion of untranslatability must be regarded as political naïveté in the most favorable construction. Finally, however, it is a reactionary move that seems likely to have no other effect than to shore up the current critical orthodoxy in academic literary and cultural studies.

This assessment becomes more convincing if we recognize that a mass protest movement, to take one form of political action, might very well be supported and expanded by various kinds of translation. The mobilization of Occupy Wall Street (ows) in New York City occurred in September 2011 in the wake of contacts with such comparable movements as the uprisings in the Arab world and the Spanish *Los Indignados*. "The People's Library" created at Zuccotti Park contained such translations as Stéphane Hessel's *Time for Outrage: Indignez-vous!* and the Invisible Committee's *The Coming Insurrection*.[92] At the same time, a cadre of indefatigable translators were translating the ows General Assembly's English-language documents into twenty-six languages, disseminating its goals and strategies and no doubt helping the movement to go global.

Yet before ows the Spanish translation of Hessel's pamphlet, *¡Indignaos!*, had been extremely important in galvanizing a political movement in Spain.[93] The translation was published in late February 2011, and by March the grassroots organization known as *¡Democracia Real Ya!* (Real Democracy Now!) had emerged to initiate the protests that occurred on May 15 in Madrid and quickly spread to other cities. The protesters called themselves *Los Indignados* (the indignant ones), after the title of the translation, although the Spanish version resonates with meanings that exceed Hessel's French.

The French title is cast in the second-person plural imperative—it might be translated into English as "Get Indignant!"—a command that constructs a position for a collective subject, a protest movement. As Matthew Harrington observes, the Spanish version maintains a correspondence with this meaning, yet it also contains shifts from the French, both phonological and grammatical.[94] The Spanish at once colloquializes and regionalizes Hessel's use of standard French by resorting to the elision of the intervocalic /d/ that occurs in Spanish-language speech, especially in Andalusia. A grammatical ambiguity is also introduced insofar as *indignados/indignaos* can be taken as either the present imperative of the verb *indignar* or the past participle, an adjectival form (hence English versions might be either "get indignant" or "the indignant ones" in the sense of "those who were made indignant").[95] The same word, then, issues a command to express indignation through protest and describes a state of being indignant with a temporal dimension, potentially encapsulating a historical narrative. Harrington explains the trajectory that the narrative might take: "once we had a kind of dignity in a democratic European welfare state which endowed us with political power in the wake of Franco's dictatorship, but we experienced the collective loss of power that attended the perceptible shift to a form of autocracy in which, through money, financial institutions wield more power than governments."[96] The possibility that Spanish readers might formulate this narrative is indicated in the preface by the Spanish economist José Luis Sampedro who points to resemblances between his life and

Hessel's: "Yo también nací en 1917. Yo también estoy indignado. También viví una guerra. También soporté una dictadura." ("I too was born in 1917. I too am indignant. I too lived through a war. I too endured a dictatorship.")[97] Sampedro can allude so obliquely to the Spanish Civil War and Franco's fascism because the economist assumes that his readers will immediately understand. In its very title the Spanish translation of Hessel's pamphlet inscribes an interpretation that constructs a distinctively Spanish political subject, speaking directly to the citizens who joined the movement.

Political action requires communication and translation, even if what translation communicates can be only an interpretation, one among other possible and competing interpretations. Translation is still a means of establishing a common ground, even if that ground is fissured with linguistic, cultural, and social differences that translation can also aim to register and negotiate. The failure of Barbara Cassin, Emily Apter, and their fellow travelers to recognize the importance of these points demonstrates the damaging cultural and political consequences that can derive from instrumental thinking about translation, especially when it underwrites a notion of untranslatability. In tending to validate particular interpretations as correct translations, this kind of thinking limits the range of meanings, values, and functions that a source text can support, removing them from scrutiny and criticism, maintaining their institutional conditions, and therefore suppressing the possibilities for cultural and social change. In the U.S. academy, the conditions include the dominance of English and English-language translations in literary and cultural studies, including curricula for world literature, so that foreign language learning is diminished in importance, and the study of translation, for which proficiency in a foreign language is essential, remains marginal. A hermeneutic understanding of translation can help to reverse this situation by enabling translations to be read as texts with their own signifying processes, related to but distinct from those of the texts they translate. The centrality of translation to academic institutions, still insufficiently acknowledged, demands that it finally be taken seriously as an object of research, teaching, and practice.

2

Proverbs of Untranslatability

Why Proverbs?

Clichés, words and phrases used repeatedly and often without much thought or inventiveness, have constituted the dominant means of understanding and commenting on translation since antiquity. The cliché may take the form of a dichotomy indicating opposed translation strategies, such as "word-for-word" vs. "sense-for-sense," which received its most influential formulation in Jerome's *Epistula LVII* (395 CE): "non verbum e verbo, sed sensum exprimere de sensu."[1] In some cases, it may develop into a fully fledged proverb about translation, a pithy statement that is believed to encapsulate an accepted truth and therefore to be worthy of repeated application, whether in elite or in popular cultures, whether by the scholar or by the general reader. In this category belong catchphrases like "traduttore traditore" and "poetry is what gets lost in translation," usually attributed to Robert Frost. Yet even Jacques Derrida's paradox— "Rein n'est intraduisible en un sens, mais *en un autre sens* tout est intraduisible" ("In a sense, nothing is untranslatable; but *in another sense* everything is untranslatable")—has now been used so many times as to risk becoming a theoretical chestnut, quoted but rarely submitted to the sort of critical examination that a philosopher like Derrida would have welcomed.[2]

Why formulaic expressions should be prevalent in translation commentary is not clear, at least initially. They are undoubtedly indicative of rote thinking. Although the repetitive use of concepts occurs in connection with other practices, it seems to be done so frequently with translation, and with such negative expressions, as to contribute to its continuing marginality. The practice attracts reductiveness, in other words, because it is assumed to be simplistic or mechanical, lacking the creative or conceptual sophistication that would require more complex explanation.

But perhaps the problem is not so much rote thinking as a dearth of ideas. George Steiner has suggested that although "the literature on the theory, practice, and history of translation is large," the fact is that "the number of original, significant ideas in the subject remains very meagre. . . . Identical theses, familiar moves and refutations in debate recur, nearly without exception, from Cicero and Quintilian to the present-day."[3] If we follow Steiner's assessment of over two millennia of translation commentary, a sheer lack of intellectual innovation has led not only to the emergence of a body of conventional wisdom, but also to an excessive reliance upon it. In the absence of new concepts, it would seem, formulaic expressions have acquired an explanatory power that merits their reiteration.

I will argue that this account is misleading. Not only does Steiner's assessment of the literature ignore significant differences across centuries of translation theory and practice, but it also fails to illuminate how translation in particular could have become dominated by rote thinking as well as what is at issue in the recourse to conventional wisdom. To provide answers to these questions, we must interrogate long-entrenched assumptions about translation that underlie proverbial statements. It will help to start with an examination of the proverb as a genre and then to return translation proverbs to the originary contexts where they were intended to express specific ideas and to serve particular rhetorical purposes. The aim is to defamiliarize notions that have come to be all too familiar as truths of translation, to show how they actually limit thinking about what translation is and does, and to indicate other, more productive directions that thinking can take. Throughout we will be especially concerned with relations between clichéd thinking and the instrumental model of translation.

The Proverb as Metaphor

The proverb is a genre riven by contradiction. On the one hand, the form is structured for maximum rhetorical effectiveness through brevity and diverse kinds of repetition—acoustic, lexical, syntactical. Linguistic features like rhyme and alliteration, metrical regularity and parallel construction produce an effect that is simultaneously mnemonic and suasive: not only do these features serve as an aid to memory, but they also, coupled with the brevity typical of proverbs, engineer a forceful closure that invests the content with the illusionistic appearance of truth, at once timeless and universal. The form of the proverb is thus characterized by invariance. The content, on the other hand, is both moralistic and disseminating: the proverb functions as a rule for conduct that rests uneasily on metaphorical substitution through potentially unlimited applications in heterogeneous contexts. As a result, the meanings of the proverb multiply without end, eventually entering into contradiction and nonsense, preempting the illusionism of the form, its truth effect. The content of the proverb is thus characterized by variance.

This contradiction between form and content makes the proverb a uniquely compelling instance of what Derrida called the *retrait* of metaphor.[4] Language is intrinsically metaphorical, including the very language that points to this intrinsic quality, so that a linguistic representation does not offer direct access to reality or truth but rather a representation mediated by a textual network.[5] This metaphoricity, however, withdraws from the language user's awareness, not least when an actual metaphor is used:

> in its withdrawal [*retrait*], one should say in its withdrawals, metaphor perhaps retires, withdraws from the worldwide scene, and does so at the moment of its most invasive extension, at the instant it overflows every limit. Its withdrawal would then have the paradoxical form of an indiscreet and overflowing insistence, of an overabundant remanence, an intrusive repetition, always marking with a supplementary trait, with one more turn, with a re-turn and *re-tracing* or *re-drawing* [re-trait] the trait that it will have left right on the text.[6]

The supplementary trait is nothing in itself, neither a literal nor a figurative meaning in a text. It is rather a movement or oscillation that can be glimpsed, in the case of the proverb, through the abstraction to which the proverb is implicitly reduced or into which it is translated, the idea that it is assumed to signify. This abstraction turns the proverb into a metaphor, or returns it to its metaphorical status, becoming the tenor to its vehicle. The trait disclosed by the abstraction is a re-trait insofar as it marks what always already exists in the proverb, its metaphoricity, which enables its endless application or further translation in heterogeneous contexts where the trait withdraws or retreats from consciousness. As Derrida observes,

> the trait remarks itself by withdrawing itself, by re-drawing itself; it succeeds in/by effacing itself in an other, in re-inscribing itself there in a parallel way, hence *heterologically*, and *allegorically*. The trait is withdrawn/re-drawn; the trait is re-trait.[7]

The proverb is heterological because the contexts where it is applied are irreducibly different, putting into question its applicability; it is allegorical because it signifies an abstraction in those contexts, which works to suppress their differences. The truth of the proverb is always figural, lacking any literal foundation in or adequacy to reality, yet its figurality is concealed first by the truth effect of its form and then by the withdrawal of the trait disclosed by the abstraction, a movement that is repeated with each new application or translation. In the proverb, form is translated into content, valorizing it; content disseminates through further translation, undoing that valorization; but form recoups it, endlessly. The proverb sets going processes of translation that transform their source materials, whether form or content, but the transformation remains invisible, unthought.

Consider, for example, the proverb, "a stitch in time saves nine." OxfordDictionaries.com translates it into the abstraction that reflects most current use: "If you sort out a problem immediately it may save a lot of extra work later." This translation turns the proverb into a metaphor, deferring its relation to any specific context while allowing it to be applied to or translated into infinite contexts. The formal features of the proverb, notably its brevity, its iambic regularity, and its rhyme, produce the forceful closure that releases an illusionistic effect of truth, which is undermined by the sheer heterogeneity of countless applications. The range of fields where "a stitch in time saves nine" is applied, judging from both popular and specialized texts accessible on the internet, includes agriculture, business, chemistry, child welfare, finance, information technology, law, medicine, mining, and psychology.

Even when surveyed within a single field, like medicine, the applications reveal such divergent meanings as to cast doubt not only on whether they bear any resemblance to each other but also on whether the proverb itself makes any sense. Thus "a stitch in time" has been used to describe both cosmetic surgery and bowel resection, both sterilization as a method of birth control and chemotherapy for advanced lung cancer.[8] Distinctions between surgical procedures that are "elective," "urgent," or "emergency" are effectively erased in these applications. Yet whether in the case of terminal illness the proverb carries much meaning at all remains questionable: if the patient's life is no more than prolonged for a limited period, the notion of saving time turns out to be empty of significance. Or take the application to premarital medical examinations, which are treated as a means "to safeguard and preserve the integrity as well as the sanctity of marriage as an institution."[9] Insofar as the article emphasizes the detection of sexually transmitted diseases, the check-up is unlikely to solve or mitigate a later marital problem but rather to preempt marriage altogether. Thomas Fuller's inclusion of the proverb in his huge compendium, *Gnomologia* (1732), seems to have anticipated the potentiality for nonsensical applications by printing a qualified formulation on two lines: "A Stitch in Time / May save nine."[10]

Translation Proverbs and Instrumentalism

When a proverb addresses the translator or translation, curiously, its relationship to the genre changes. The formal invariance may persist, whether through brevity or a repetitive structure or a combination of these features. When put to use, furthermore, the proverb is still reduced to or translated into an abstraction, which discloses its metaphoricity. Yet the content is not variable: the proverb does not undergo an unlimited range of applications or translations in heterogeneous contexts. The context is always the same, the practice of translation, whether generalized to every time and place or applicable to a specific case. And in every application, at least from the twentieth century onward, the proverb signifies the same basic meaning: untranslatability, or the impossibility of translation.

Consider "traduttore traditore." Even though the proverb is

Italian, the plural version ("Traduttori traditori") was included in editions of the *Oxford Dictionary of English Proverbs* between 1935 and 1970 before appearing in more general reference works, a fact that attests to its widespread use in Anglophone writing.[11] The *Dictionary* adds a translation into English, "Translators, traitors," along with several illustrative passages that date from the seventeenth to the twentieth centuries. One passage, drawn from a 1929 letter to the editor of the London *Times*, explains how "personal visits to buyers abroad" lead to successful trade relations with foreign countries. But the visitor is advised not to rely on translation: "The visitor . . . ought to be able to speak fluently the language of the country visited. Working through an interpreter is roundabout and in many cases hopeless. As the Italian proverb says: *Traduttore traditore.*"[12]

This use of the proverb shows it functioning in line with the genre, although with a significant deviation. It is employed as a conclusive explanation whose cogency is enforced by brevity, repetitive rhythm, and paronomasia. It is also reduced to an abstract meaning, namely that translation is impossible ("hopeless"), which turns it into a metaphorical vehicle for this idea and enables its application to interpreting in commercial transactions. Yet at this stage the proverb stops functioning as such: it lacks the proliferation and dissemination of meaning that typify the genre. The specificity of the context does not involve any further metaphorical substitution, any particular application to commerce or to interpreting. The proverb merely asserts the failure of translation, as if untranslatability were a timeless and universal truth. Although it is moralistic, moreover, it offers no viable rule for conduct except, implicitly, a rejection of translation. The translator is doomed to fail because of the very nature of translation, a point that is driven home by the acoustic similarity between "traduttore" and "traditore." The pun indicates that translation and treachery are one and the same.

Some uses of this proverb can be more revealing of the theoretical assumptions on which it rests. Arthur Sze, a contemporary Chinese American poet, cites it in the introduction to his translations of Chinese poetry:

> I know translation is an "impossible" task, and I have never forgotten the Italian phrase *traduttori/traditori*: "translators/ traitors." Which translation does not in some way betray its original? In considering the process of my own translations, I am aware of loss and transformation, of destruction and renewal.[13]

Although Sze puts the word "impossible" within skeptical quotation marks, he nonetheless reduces the proverb to the idea that translation is impossible when he asks the rhetorical question, "Which translation does not in some was betray its original?" The implicit answer, of course, is none. He then offers a glimpse of what "betray" might mean in this context through such general terms as "loss," "transformation," "destruction," and "renewal," all of which imply that the translator is trusted to leave the source text unchanged, but this trust is always betrayed insofar as translation necessarily causes change.

Sze's remarks point to an instrumental model of translation: they imagine translation as the reproduction or transfer of an invariant contained in the source text, an essential form or meaning which the translator ought to preserve intact but never does because of the transformative nature of translation. The proverb assumes but paradoxically forestalls the viability of instrumentalism. Thus the formal and semantic invariance of "traduttore traditore," the punning proverb that refers only to translation, seems to be a reflection or projection of a more fundamental concept, the assumption of formal and semantic invariance that is thought to characterize the source text. All the same, invariance is invoked only to be disallowed. Perhaps

"traduttore traditore," after all, does resemble such other proverbs as "a stitch in time saves nine": although the translation
proverb stops short of endless metaphorical substitution, an
interrogation of its theoretical assumptions reveals that it too
devolves into contradiction and nonsense.

When the proverb is cited in translation commentary that is
more theoretically sophisticated, different models of translation
might be put into play. At the end of "On Linguistic Aspects
of Translation" (1959), Roman Jakobson introduces "traduttore
traditore" into his discussion of the untranslatability of poetry:

> The pun, or to use a more erudite, and perhaps more precise
> term—paronomasia, reigns over poetic art, and whether its
> rule is absolute or limited, poetry by definition is untrans-
> latable. Only creative transposition is possible: either
> intralingual transposition—from one poetic shape into
> another, or interlingual transposition—from one language
> into another, or finally intersemiotic transposition—from
> one system of signs into another, e.g., from verbal art into
> music, dance, cinema, or painting.
>
> If we were to translate into English the traditional formula
> *Traduttore, traditore* as "the translator is a betrayer," we would
> deprive the Italian rhyming epigram of all its paronomastic
> value. Hence a cognitive attitude would compel us to change
> this aphorism into a more explicit statement and to answer
> the questions: translator of what messages? betrayer of what
> values?[14]

Remarkably, Jakobson's comments assume two, mutually exclusive models of translation. On the one hand is instrumentalism.
This assumption is first implied by his notion that poetry is
"untranslatable" and then exemplified by his treatment of the
proverb: he uses it to illustrate the impossibility of reproducing what he takes to be a formal invariant, "its paronomastic

value," while tacitly demonstrating the truth of the proverb. Thus both poetry and proverb are untranslatable because they contain invariant features that translation should reproduce or transfer but fails to do so insofar as the nature of translation is to change the source text. On the other hand, however, Jakobson also assumes a quite different hermeneutic model of translation: it regards translation as an interpretation that inevitably varies the form and meaning of the source text according to the translating language or medium. Hence he proposes to solve the problem of untranslatability by resorting to "creative transposition," which involves various kinds of changes—in "poetic shape," in "language," or in "system of signs." Yet the term "creative transposition" is misleading because Jakobson refers to the same process as "translation" at the beginning of his essay, where he first distinguishes among "three ways of interpreting a verbal sign":

1. Intralingual translation or *rewording* is an interpretation of verbal signs by means of other signs of the same language.
2. Interlingual translation or *translation proper* is an interpretation of verbal signs by means of some other language.
3. Intersemiotic translation or *transmutation* is an interpretation of verbal signs by means of signs of nonverbal sign systems.[15]

Beneath the seemingly coherent exposition of Jakobson's essay slide two contradictory models of translation: one instrumental, stressing invariance, reproduction or transfer, and untranslatability; the other hermeneutic, stressing variation, interpretation, and translatability. The comment on the "cognitive attitude" with which he closes the essay does not actually resolve this contradiction since it can support both models (despite the fact that he considers this attitude the basis of an alternative translation of the proverb). If the "messages" and "values" that are translated or betrayed are viewed as formal and thematic invariants contained in the proverb or derived from its application to a particular case of translation, then the "cognitive attitude" would assume the instrumental model, although with the difference that the "more explicit" translation would be capable of communicating those invariants and hence validating instrumentalism. If the "messages" and "values" are viewed as the result of an interpretation inscribed in the proverb or its application, one among various possible interpretations that fix its form and theme, then the "cognitive attitude" would assume the hermeneutic model, and the translation that transforms the proverb into a "more explicit statement" would be capable of communicating that interpretation to the exclusion of others.

This indeterminacy shows that the distinction between instrumental and hermeneutic models of translation may seem to form a binary opposition, but on further scrutiny any such opposition collapses to reveal the primacy of interpretation and its constitutive role in thinking about translation. Both models are heuristic in understanding what translation is and does, they are models in the sense of conceptual constructions, and so instrumentalism too can be seen as a set of theoretical assumptions that underlie or give rise to a particular interpretation of translation practice. Yet the impact of instrumentalist assumptions, both intellectual and practical, is costly. The assumption of formal and semantic invariance breaks off thinking about translation in the same way that it breaks off, in the case of translation proverbs, the proliferation and dissemination of meaning that typify the proverb genre. Instrumentalism, to be more precise, preempts thinking about translation as an interpretive act that varies the source text, suppressing the assumption of a hermeneutic model of translation that can take into account this variance.

A Genealogy of "Traduttore Traditore"

The terms "traduttore" and "traditore" are linked as a tendentious analogy in the early modern period. Initially presented in an expository form, the analogy quickly hardens into a proverb with paronomastic force. Over several centuries the proverb accumulates various meanings that develop and nuance the notion of betrayal in translation while consistently assuming an instrumental model. These meanings can be divided into two categories, one satirical, targeting translators thought to be incompetent, the other philosophical, asserting a metaphysical basis for untranslatability. In some contexts, both meanings are in play, with one functioning as the explanation or justification of the other.

What seems to be the first formulation occurs in *Le pistole vulgari* (1539), a collection of letters by the poet and satirist Niccolò Franco.[16] The passage appears in an invective against various professions:

Veggo in un altro cantone, I TRADUTTORI, li quali tal che mostrino al volgo, & a chi non sa, di sapere due lettere, traducono l'opre da la latina ne la lingua volgare. Veggo quando per non intender bene il testo de gli autori, danno giù di mostaccio. Veggo quando distillano fino al grasso de le lor barbe per trovare un vocaboluccio ne i rifugi de i commentari. E per che gli veggo morire con tutte le lor fatiche da quell'ora che le cominciano, per la pietà grande che me ne viene, non posso far che non dica: Ser Traditori miei, se non sapete far'altro che tradire i libri, voi ve ne anderete bel bello a cacare senza candela.[17]

In another corner, I see THE TRANSLATORS, who just to show the common people, & whoever doesn't know, that they know two literatures, translate works from Latin into the vernacular. I see them pulling an ugly mug when they don't understand the authors' text. I see them concentrating down to the grease of their beards to find a measly word in the shelter of commentaries. And because I see them dying from all their labors at the very moment they begin, because of the enormous pity that comes over me from it, I can't help saying: my Esteemed Traitors, if you can't do anything but betray books, you'll slowly go shit without a candle.

Franco's remarks assume not that translation is impossible, but that a translator must be knowledgeable. His satiric object is not all translators or translation in general, but a particular group of humanist translators (they work from Latin into the vernacular). He ridicules them for translating texts they do not understand and for using translation as a pretentious display of linguistic knowledge so as to impress the uneducated. The significance of his reference to "cacare senza candela" ("shit without a candle") seems to be both literal and figurative: not only do these translators soil rather than illuminate their Latin source texts, but the poor quality of their work will ultimately impoverish them so that they cannot afford a candle.

Interestingly, Franco's use of the analogy between translators and traitors coincides with his effort to suppress the idea that translation is an interpretive act. He derides translators whose limited knowledge of Latin forces them to rely on "i refugi de i commentari" ("the shelter of commentaries"). His remarks imply that knowledge of the source language is the sole criterion of translator competence, and that any reliance on interpretations articulated independently in commentary leads to error. Thus the source text is thought to contain a semantic invariant that is immediately accessible to the qualified translator, and the task of translation is to reproduce or transfer that invariant intact.

The analogy appeared again within a few decades of Franco's

satire. The French humanist scholar and printer Henri Estienne cited it in his *Apologie pour Hérodote* (1566), a French adaptation of his Latin text, *Apologia pro Herodoto*, which he published the same year in his edition of Herodotus. In a preface to a friend, Estienne explains that he decided to write the adaptation himself because some years ago an incompetent translator had prepared a faulty French translation of another Latin text of his. The passage below is drawn from the 1592 French edition which became the basis of Richard Carew's 1608 English version, *A World of Wonders*:

> Il ne fut plustost publié qu'il rencontra un traducteur, lequel (comme je pense) besongna tres bien à son gré & à son contentement, mais bien loin du mien, & vrayement aussi loin qu'il s'estoit eslongné de mes conceptions, lesquelles je ne pouvois recognoistre en icelle, de forte qu'il me sembloit que j'avois bien occasion de dire comme l'Italien, à-sçavoir qu'il n'avoit pas fait office de traduttore, mais de traditore. Ce que toutesfois je luy ay pardonné, qui que ce soit (car il n'y a pas mis son nom) pource que je ne doute point qu'en faisíant mal il n'ait faict du mieux qu'il a pu.[18]

> I had no sooner published a little Pamphlet, but it met with a tinkerly translator, who Pigmalion-like doted upon his owne doings, thinking he had put out the Popes eye; whereas to my thinking he roved at random, and erred the whole heavens, in such sort that I could neither conceive what I had written, nor yet perceive any footsteps of my wonted stile. So that I may well say with the *Italian*, that he performed not the office of a *traduttore*, but of a *traditore*, that is, that he played not the part of a *translator*, but of a *traitor*. Which notwithstanding I pardoned in that namelesse author, not doubting but that in doing amisse he did his best endevour.[19]

Estienne agrees with Franco that translation is possible, but he refines the Italian satirist's view. Translation competence is described more precisely as the ability to render the source author's intended meaning ("mes conceptions") which the translator betrays by translating instead according to his personal preferences ("à son gré & à son contentement"). Estienne's assumption of an instrumental model adds authorial intentionality to the semantic invariant that the translator must reproduce, although like Franco he believes that the translator in question lacked sufficient knowledge or skill to produce an effective translation.

The most notable feature of this case, however, is not so much Estienne's reference to the analogy as the contradiction between his avowed instrumentalism and Richard Carew's aggressively interpretive English version. Carew applied a concept of equivalence that might be described as lexicographical, maintaining a semantic correspondence according to definitions that can be found in contemporary dictionaries such as Jean Nicot's *Thresor de la langue françoyse, tant ancienne que moderne* (1606) and Randle Cotgrave's *A Dictionarie of the French and English Tongues* (1611).[20] Yet while establishing an equivalence Carew also translated with latitude, departing widely from Estienne's lexicon and syntax, aiming for greater explicitness to the point of redundancy and exaggeration, and interpolating suggestive words and phrases that convey meanings absent from the French text. The result is a mixture of translation and adaptation.

For instance, Estienne's account of his questionable translator—"il s'estoit eslongné de mes conceptions, lesquelles je ne pouvois recognoistre en icelle"—might be translated closely as "he deviated from my ideas, which I could not recognize in [the translation]." Carew's version is rhetorically elaborate: "to my thinking he roved at random, and erred the whole heavens, in such sort that I could neither conceive what I had written, nor yet perceive any footsteps of my wonted stile." As a result, Carew includes a formal invariant—the author's "wonted stile"—with the intended meaning that Estienne thought should be reproduced in a translation.

Carew undoubtedly shared, even as he expanded, Estienne's instrumentalism. His preface to his translation asserts not only that "I have expressed the meaning of my author both truly and fully," but also that "I have not lost either the life or the grace of any conceit, where it was possible to be kept," implying that for the most part he reproduced the stylistic features of the French text, "the life or the grace" with which Estienne's "conceit" or "meaning" is signified.[21] Carew does not explain the qualification, "where it was possible to be kept," but his subsequent reference to "those infinite rubs that lay in my way" suggests that the potential hindrances may have been the peculiarities of Estienne's style combined with the structural differences between French and English and the translator's own linguistic deficiency: "I do not professe my self a Translator," he states, "neither do I arrogate any extraordinary skil in the French language."[22] In the same passage, Carew describes his translation as "the gay coate that I have put upon" the French text, whereby he glances at his embellishments while simultaneously indicating that they do not compromise his transfer of formal and semantic invariants. The clothing metaphor, so frequent in the early modern period, reflects Carew's instrumentalism insofar as it denies that "a translation can seriously change the substance of the original."[23]

Nonetheless, Carew's verbal choices do in fact introduce substantive differences. They show him inscribing an interpretation that exceeds any equivalence, whether stylistic or lexicographical, thereby transforming the form and meaning of the French text. Carew constructed a complicated image of Estienne's French translator, which starts with a more explicitly

pejorative assessment of his limitations as "tinkerly," an early
modern usage meaning "clumsy, bungling, unskillful" (*OED*),
and then assigns motives that join pride ("Pigmalion-like [he]
doted upon his owne doings") with militant Protestantism.
The phrase, "thinking he had put out the Popes eye," may refer
to a cut of meat "regarded as a delicacy" (*OED*), serving as a
metaphor for the translator's self-satisfaction, or it may refer
to his investment in the nature of Estienne's text, a harsh satire
of the Catholic Church. Carew's verbal choices, perhaps his
very decision to translate Estienne's satire, seem directed to
an English readership who has the Gunpowder Plot fresh in
their minds, the Catholic conspiracy against James I foiled in
1605. Hence Carew dated his preface, "Novemb.7.Anno 1607,"
adding "the day after the gun powder Treason."[24]

His address to a Jacobean audience is also apparent in the
proliferation of idiomatic expressions that lack any correspondence to the French text. Phrases like "rove at random," "err the
whole heavens," even the allusion to the Pygmalion myth recur
in original compositions during the sixteenth and seventeenth
centuries. Sir William Cornwallis's essay, "Of Suspicion," published not long before Carew's translation, includes the same
mythological allusion with the same negative force: "Who seeth
a Lover, & loves not? forcing his imagination to draw a portra-
ture of perfection, and then Pigmalion-like inamoured of his
owne workemanship, and laughes not?"[25] Carew's translation
assimilated Estienne's text to contemporary Anglophone values,
both linguistic and cultural. This strategy led him to anglicize
geographical markers as well: he points out that he rendered the
phrase, "Entre Paris & Lyon," as "betwixt Yorke & London."[26]

The contradiction that Carew's version opens up between
instrumental and hermeneutic models of translation is strik-
ingly encapsulated in his handling of Estienne's reference to
the Italian analogy. Again mindful of his English-speaking

readers, Carew not only translated Estienne's French sentence but also inserted a translation of the Italian words themselves. The English version of Estienne's sentence, "he performed not the office of a *traduttore*, but of a *traditore*," relies on another idiomatic expression that was used with great frequency in early modern English, "perform the office of," where "office" carries the meaning of "a duty attaching to a person's station, position, or employment" (OED). This ethical sense of "office" is consistent with instrumentalism, the assumption that a translator's duty is to reproduce a source-text invariant, appropriately signified through the use of a French borrowing ("office") in the English translation of a French text. Yet when Carew translated the Italian analogy—"he played not the part of a *translator*, but of a *traitor*"—he introduced a different but equally familiar idiom, "play the part of," which carries the meaning of "to act as or like" (OED). This idiom signifies a rather different conception of the translator as an actor who can take on a succession of roles, signaling the assumption that translation offers an interpretation that varies the source text. One can act as either a translator or a traitor, in other words, although being a translator is itself like being an actor of changing roles as opposed to an officer with a fixed duty. This point would have been particularly discernible to readers who were also theatergoers, since on the Jacobean stage "most players would have been expected to have a range of performing styles," and, "as frequently happened, one actor played distinct roles in the same play."[27] The address to an Anglophone readership seems to have run counter to Carew's claim of equivalence, such that his change of idiom transformed the theoretical assumptions underlying Estienne's text.

A Metaphysics of Translation

The early modern period also saw the use of the Italian analogy to speculate on the conditions of untranslatability, although without entirely abandoning its satirical value. Joachim du Bellay's *Défense et illustration de la langue française* (1549) presents a French version, referring to "traducteurs" who are "traditeurs" so as to ridicule precisely the sort of incompetence and pretentiousness that provoked Franco. Yet du Bellay quickly shifts his attention to what makes translation impossible:

Mais que diray-je d'aucuns, vrayement mieux dignes d'estre appellés traditeurs que traducteurs? Veu qu'ilz trahissent ceux qu'ilz entreprennent exposer, les frustrant de leur gloire, et par mesme moyen seduysent les lecteurs ignorans, leur montrant le blanc pour le noyr: qui, pour acquerir le nom de sçavans, traduysent à credict les langues, dont jamais ilz n'ont entendu les premiers elementz, comme l'Hebraique et la Grecque: et encor' pour myeux se faire valoir, se prennent aux poëtes, genre d'aucteurs certes auquel si je sçavoy', ou vouloy' traduyre, je m'adroisseroy' aussi peu, à cause de ceste divinité d'invention qu'ilz ont plus que les autres, de ceste grandeur de style, magnificence de motz, gravité de sentences, audace et varieté de figures, et mil'autres lumieres de poësie: bref ceste energie, et ne sçay quel esprit, qui est en leurs ecriz, que les Latins appelleroient *genius*. Toutes les quelles choses se peuvent autant exprimer en traduisant, comme un peintre peut représenter l'ame avecques le corps de celuy qu'il entreprend tyrer apres le naturel.

But what shall I say of some who truly deserve rather to be called traitors than translators? For they betray those they undertake to reveal, denying them their glory and by the same means seduce ignorant readers, showing them white for black. To gain the name of learned men, they translate on credit languages, like Hebrew and Greek, of which they have never understood the first elements and to raise their standing still further, take on poets, a race of authors that, if I could or would translate, I would address as little as possible because of that divinity of invention they have more than others, that greatness of style, magnificence of words, gravity of thoughts, boldness and variety of figures, and a thousand other adornments of poetry; in short, that energy and indefinable spirit in their writings which the Latins would call *genius.* All these things can be no more rendered in translation than a painter can represent the soul along with the body of the person he undertakes to portray from life.[28]

For du Bellay, the translators in question are traitors not simply because their limited knowledge of the source languages renders them incompetent but also because they attempt to translate what is untranslatable. He observes that poetry possesses this quality more than other kinds of writing ("plus que les autres"), suggesting that it can be found in all writing to some degree. Formal features ("invention," "style," "motz," "sentences," "figures") constitute a spiritual essence ("energie," "esprit," "genius") which cannot be translated. Du Bellay's use of the Latin word "genius" to signify this form-based essence synthesizes various meanings that date back to antiquity and circulate in France in the early sixteenth century, including "tutelary spirit," "taste" or "inclination," and "talent."[29] Not only does the essence seem to be inherent in the poet as well as in the poetry (it is said to be endemic to poets as a particular "genre" or genus of author), but du Bellay also regards it as an invariant that transcends the contingencies of time and place, comparable to divinity.[30] Hence he asserts that translation can "profaner ainsi les sacrées reliques de l'Antiquité" ("profane the sacred remains of antiquity") which are clearly thought to retain their sanctity for readers of classical languages in his historical moment.[31] Du Bellay's concept of writing amounts to a secular religion that assigns a metaphysical basis to untranslatability.

To formulate this view, he must at once assume and repudiate an instrumental model of translation. Thus he locates source-text invariants that the translator would need to reproduce or transfer—if the translator were faithful rather than traitorous and if translation were possible. These invariants relate to textual form, but they also include its effect upon the reader. Du Bellay imagines that readers of ancient Greek and Latin texts experience the same emotional response to those texts, regardless of the time and place of their reading, and this response ought to be reproduced or transferred—if the translator were faithful rather than traitorous and if translation were possible:

> il est impossible de le rendre avecques la mesme grace dont l'autheur en a usé: d'autant que chaque langue a je ne sçay quoy propre seulement à elle, dont si vous efforcez exprimer le naif dans une autre langue, observant la loy de traduyre, qui est n'espacer point hors des limites de l'aucteur, vostre diction sera contrainte, froide et de mauvaise grace. Et qu'ainsi soit, qu'on me lyse un Demosthene et Homere Latins, un Ciceron et Vergile Français, pour voir s'ilz vous engendreront telles affections, voyre ainsi qu'un Prothée vous transformeront en diverses sortes, comme vous sentez, lysant ces aucteurs en leurs langues.

> it is impossible to render a work with the same grace that the author put into it, inasmuch as each language has an indescribable something that belongs to it alone, so that if you try to express its inborn quality in another language, abiding by the law of translation, which is never to stray beyond the bounds of the author, your diction will be constrained, cold, and graceless. And as proof, just read a Latin Demosthenes and Homer, a French Cicero and Virgil, to see if they will beget such emotions in you—will, indeed, transform you like a Proteus into differing kinds—as you feel reading those authors in their own languages.[32]

In this passage, du Bellay uses terms like "grace," "je ne sçay quoy," and "naif," but their significance is virtually the same as that of the terms I have already quoted, namely "energie," "ne sçay quel esprit," and "genius": they all indicate a spiritual essence, stemming from the formal features of a text. Nicot's dictionary entry for "naif," in fact, includes "genuinus," a Latin word meaning "innate" which like "genius" derives from "gigno," "to beget, bear, bring forth, produce."[33] Du Bellay assumes the instrumental model in citing a number of formal and affective invariants contained in or caused by the source text, but then he eliminates their materiality by transforming them into a transcendental property. This property can be made the basis of untranslatability because it is described as resisting precise definition and even cognition ("ne sçay quell," "je ne sçay quoy"). Yet du Bellay insists that any reader can perceive it simply by reading a text in the language in which it was originally written.

How can a translator not betray the source text if the measure of effective translation is the reproduction or transfer of an indefinable quality said to be divine? The reader, meanwhile, who experiences the "divinité d'invention" or "genius" of the original composition is likewise deified, passively turned into a Proteus through an emotional response that changes from one text to another but is unaffected by temporal and spatial coordinates (as might be expected of a god). Neither reading nor translation is conceived as an interpretive act performed on a linguistic artifact.

This suppression of the hermeneutic comes back to worry du Bellay's effort to distinguish between different kinds of translators and translation practices. As critics have noted, he uses two sets of terms in commenting on translation: "traducteur," "traduction," and "traduire" vs. "translateur," "translation," "translater."[34] The first set he applies to translation that maintains a semantic correspondence to the source text, at least as practiced by "fideles traducteurs" ("faithful translators") instead of "traditeurs."[35] Hence he commends "l'office et diligence des traducteurs" as "fort utiles pour instruire les ignorans des langues étrangères en la connaissance des choses" ("the diligent service of translators [as] very useful in instructing those ignorant of foreign languages in the knowledge of things"): such instruction could not occur without the communication of source-text meaning, conceived as an invariant that does not require interpretation to be conveyed.[36] Similarly, he sees these translators as avoiding poetry and oratory and rather focusing on "autres parties de literature, et ce rond de sciences que les Grecz ont nommé encyclopedie" ("other kinds of writing and that cycle of learned disciplines that the Greeks called the 'encyclopedia'").[37] Du Bellay implies that texts in other literary genres as well as in scholarly disciplines place less emphasis on form than on meaning, which the "fidele traducteur" can reproduce or transfer.

To the translator who emphasizes formal features he applies the second set of terms, signifying a different translation practice. Yet his application is inconsistent, since he recommends that the "translateur" take this approach with philosophical texts, not poetry and oratory:

> seroy' je bien d'opinion que le sçavant translateur fist plus tost l'office de paraphraste que de traducteur, s'efforceant donner à toutes les sciences qu'il voudra traiter l'ornement et lumiere de sa langue, comme Ciceron se vante d'avoir fait en la phylosophie, et à l'exemple des Italiens, qui l'ont quasi toute convertie en leur vulgaire, principalement la Platonique.

> I would be of the opinion that the learned translator should perform rather the role of a paraphraser than of word-for-word translator, striving to give to all the disciplines he wishes to treat the ornament and light of his language, as

Cicero boasts of having done in philosophy, and following the example of the Italians who have converted nearly all of it into their vulgar tongue, especially Platonic philosophy.[38]

In likening the work of the "translateur" to that of the "paraphraste," du Bellay links translation to interpretation. Nicot's dictionary defines "paraphrase" as "exposition et interpretation qui ne se fait point de mot pour mot, ains de sentence pour sentence" (exposition and interpretation that is not done word for word, but sense for sense). Nicot's entry bears out the decision of du Bellay's translator, Richard Helgerson, to insert the phrase "word-for-word" to describe the "traducteur," who would seem to construe the meaning of the source text by taking the individual word as the unit of translation. This unit helps to clarify what du Bellay denotes by "la loy de traduyre, qui est n'espacer point hors des limites de l'aucteur" ("the law of translation, which is never to stray beyond the bounds of the author"). The paraphrastic "translateur," in contrast, interprets the meaning of the source text by taking larger (unspecified) linguistic units, rewriting them in the most attractive style in the translating language, its "ornament et lumiere" ("ornament and light").

Still, might not this rewriting, insofar as it assimilates the source text to the linguistic values of a different culture, exceed the "limites de l'aucteur," affecting the interpretation to such an extent that the "translateur" also risks becoming a "traditeur"? And does not the "fidele traducteur" also offer an interpretation by focusing on each source-language word in an effort to fix their meaning with words in the translating language? As soon as the issue of interpretation enters the discussion, it undermines du Bellay's assumption of an instrumental model of translation and ultimately collapses the distinctions he tries to draw between kinds of translators and translation practices.

By the nineteenth century, the Italian proverb came to be listed in compendia like Giuseppe Giusti's *Proverbi toscani* (1873), although it bears no specific affiliation to Tuscany, and Robert Christy's *Proverbs, Maxims and Phrases of All Ages* (1888), where it was presented only in English.[39] Occasionally, the citation exceeded mere listing and involved commentary. In 1853 Richard Chenevix Trench, an Anglican archbishop who wrote on philological as well as theological topics, cited the Italian proverb to illustrate the formal features of the genre. "In a remarkable manner," he found, it

> unites all three qualities of which we have been last treating, brevity, rhyme, and alliteration: *Traduttori, traditori*; one which we might perhaps reconstitute in English thus: *Translators, traitors*; so untrue, for the most part, are they to the genius of their original, to its spirit, if not to its letter, and frequently to both; so do they *surrender*, rather than *render*, its meaning; not *turning*, but only *overturning*, it from one language to another.[40]

Trench is so taken with the form of the proverb that he imitates it by devising his own paronomasia. Although he gives no reason why translators are "so untrue," he does explain the nature of their treachery by relying on the metaphysical grounding that du Bellay had first formulated. Trench's reference to "genius," however, lacks the French poet's sacralization, stopping at the assumption of a text-based essence and linking it to another, equally metaphysical cliché of translation commentary, "spirit" vs. "letter," what Antoine Berman called the "Platonic figure of translating" that distinguishes between "spirit and letter, sense and word, content and form, the sensible and the nonsensible."[41] Hence Trench aligns "genius" and "spirit" with the "meaning" of the source text, revealing his instrumentalism in the charge that translators fail to "render" a semantic invariant.

The Italian proverb continued to be cited repeatedly into

the twentieth century and beyond in both popular and academic publications. The applications remained extraordinarily consistent, as commentators used it either to describe translator incompetence or to assert the impossibility of translation, often both at the same time. Whenever the proverb introduced extended analyses of translations, however, the instrumentalism on which it rested led to a lack of critical self-consciousness. The more learned the commentary, in fact, the more the commentator seemed unaware of the assumptions that enabled the application of the proverb.

In 1952, for instance, the poet-translator John Frederick Nims published a scathing review in *Poetry* magazine entitled "Traduttore, Traditore: Campbell's St. John of the Cross," in which he savaged Roy Campbell's English translation of the Spanish poet's work. Campbell's version "gives some idea, more or less accurate, of the content of the poetry," writes Nims, "but it gives no idea whatsoever of the properly poetic: those qualities of imagery, diction, and rhythm that make the author one of the finest poets of any literature."[42] Nims articulated precisely the distinction between "content" and "poetry" that drove du Bellay to use the proverb, although apparently without any suggestion of metaphysics, making no mention of "genius" or "spirit." Yet this appearance is deceptive, since Nims actually does construct a metaphysical essence that he regards as inherent in the source text. Thus at the start of his review he states that "I am concerned with the poetry as poetry. (Dámaso Alonso has written a magnificent study of it in his *La poesía de San Juan de la Cruz*, Madrid, 1942.)," and at the end he concludes with a similar invocation of the Spanish scholar:

Campbell writes so glibly he has the air of being triumphant—whereas he is continually misrepresenting the poetry of St. John, with its *frescura, virginalidad, originalidad, condensación,*

intensidad, *velocidad*, *desnudez*—these are some of the words
Dámaso Alonso uses in trying to give its essential qualities.
Not one of them comes through in the Campbell translation.[43]

Nims assumes an instrumental model of translation: the Spanish
poems contain "essential qualities," a set of formal invariants that
the translator must reproduce or transfer; otherwise he betrays
the source texts. Despite his references to Alonso's scholarship,
despite his quotation of the Spanish scholar's terminology, Nims
shows no awareness that he has inscribed an interpretation in
the Spanish poems, that these poems might support multiple
and conflicting interpretations, especially when the interpretive
act is performed in an English translation, or that Campbell,
for whatever reason, may have chosen to develop a different
interpretation through his translating. As a result, although
Nims juxtaposes quotations of the Spanish and English, his
judgment can hardly be described as based on direct, unmediated
comparisons between the translations and the source texts. He
has rather compared Campbell's work to Alonso's account of
the Spanish poems, which he has taken as absolute, but which
can be no more than consistent with his own interpretation, a
matter of personal preference.

Poetry + Translation = Loss?

The statement attributed to Robert Frost, "poetry is what is lost
in translation," has been repeated so frequently as to become
proverbial in translation commentary. Sometimes given more
colloquially as "poetry is what gets lost in translation," it is
pointedly phrased and rhythmical, bearing a formal resemblance to proverbs, even though it lacks the rhetorical force of
"traduttore traditore." The statement also works like a proverb:
when cited, it is reduced to an abstraction that discloses its
status as a metaphor.

Yet even before citation releases that abstraction the word "lost" itself is metaphorical. Where exactly is the loss supposed to occur? The source text, if it contains "poetry," never loses that feature: despite being translated, it continues to exist intact without deprivation or destruction. Nothing can be lost from the translated text, of course, if the "poetry" never appeared there in the first place. The notion that the loss occurs during the translation process, the meaning that is usually assigned to the statement, constitutes a metaphor for nontranslation or omission, although it neither describes nor explains what brings about these potential results. The metaphor of loss is moralistic but unaccountable: it already conceals some concept of what translation is and ought to do, yet without making that concept explicit or allowing it to be inferred with any precision apart from specific contexts.

Most citations assume that the statement is self-explanatory, however, regardless of whether it is accepted or rejected. Some add interpretations that articulate what the commentators treat as an implicit abstraction. Usually, the interpretation is intended to specify the source-text properties that are lost.

In a review of poetry translations, the British poet Christopher Reid agreed with Frost's statement—"it is hard," he wrote, "to argue against that verdict"—and then proceeded to elucidate it by conceiving of poetry as a metaphysical essence: "We like to think that a poem, if it has any value, possesses a quiddity for which no other arrangement of words, let alone those in a foreign language, can be a sufficient substitute."[44] David Damrosch, in theorizing "world literature" as "writing that gains in translation," resisted metaphysical thinking like Reid's, assigning Frost's statement to "purist views of literary language" and taking it as a reference to the difficulty of translating prosody: "whatever meaning a new language can convey is irretrievably sundered from the verbal music of the original."[45] Damrosch too accepted Frost's statement, although he sought to qualify it: "It is more accurate to say that *some* works are not translatable without substantial loss, and so they remain largely within their local or national context, never achieving an effective life as world literature."[46] It would seem, then, that world literature cannot be reliably defined by reference to translated texts— the prospect of suffering "substantial loss" need not prevent a text from being translated into multiple languages and thereby worlded—but also that the category of "world literature" appears less inclusive of poetry than other genres. Citations such as those by Reid and Damrosch aim to specify or refine what Frost said, but they nonetheless show that the metaphor of loss signifies the same basic meaning in every use: poetry is untranslatable, whether completely or in varying degrees.

As with the Italian proverb, returning Frost's statement to its originary contexts can help to expose its theoretical assumptions. In a 1964 lecture, Louis Untermeyer, a long-time friend of Frost's, reported the poet using it in a conversation. Untermeyer does not date the conversation, but he observes that Frost was expressing his distaste for an extended analysis of his poem, "Stopping by Woods on a Snowy Evening," which was first published in 1923. According to Untermeyer, Frost declared: "You've often heard me say—perhaps too often—that poetry is what is lost in translation. It is also what is lost in interpretation."[47] This report makes clear that Frost did not regard translation as an interpretive act. On the contrary, he saw "translation" and "interpretation" as two distinctly different practices that can be performed on a poem. In his view, both practices are deeply questionable because they entail an omission of "poetry," a term that he did not define on this occasion.

Since Untermeyer's quotation seems to have been made from memory, the extent to which he may have edited or revised what Frost actually said remains unclear. The possibility of revision is raised by an interview Frost gave to Cleanth Brooks and Robert Penn Warren in 1959. Here, in a transcription of a tape recording that was designed to accompany the third edition of Brooks and Warren's textbook anthology, *Understanding Poetry* (1960), Frost makes a similar statement about translation, but it is much less pointed and much more vague:

> I like to say, guardedly, that I could define poetry this way: It is that which is lost out of prose and verse in translation. That means something in the way words are curved and all that— the way the words are taken, the way you take the words.[48]

In response, Warren invoked Samuel Taylor Coleridge's "best-order notion," the idea recorded in the British poet's *Table Talk* that "prose = words in the best order;—poetry = the *best* words in the best order."[49] Frost seemed to agree with Warren—he replied, "Yes, I'm pretty extreme about it"—but he did not take up the Coleridgean reference at all. This neglect should perhaps not come as a surprise: the introduction of Coleridge lacks any direct connection to Frost's comments and effectively masks their various implications.

Frost, unlike Coleridge, saw "poetry" as a formal feature of both "prose and verse." Whether this feature is inherent in language or embedded there by the author is not sharply distinguished in his phrase, "something in the way words are curved." Nor does the rest of Frost's comment clarify the point. In the repetitive phrase, "the way the words are taken, the way you take the words," each instance of the word "take" may mean both "selected and arranged by the author" and "understood or grasped by the author and reader." On the one hand, then, "poetry" may be inherent in language, an unchanging essence exploited by the author and perceptible to the reader; on the other hand, it may be an effect that depends for its very existence on the author's or reader's particular understanding of language, allowing for the possibility of a response that is not poetic, but that remains the same when that response is poetic (this idealist alternative seems inconsistent with Frost's thinking, as we shall see below). The remarkable thing is that neither concept of "poetry" affects Frost's idea that translation entails omission. Whether "poetry" is an essence inherent in the source text or an effect dependent on cognition, he treated it as an invariant that could not be reproduced or transferred in another language. Hence his belief in untranslatability assumes an instrumental model of translation.

Frost seems to have voiced his famous statement later in his career, but to understand his instrumentalism we must examine the poetics he formulated decades earlier. In letters written to friends between 1913 and 1915, he described the formal feature that defined poetry, in both verse and prose, as fundamentally prosodic, using terms such as "the sound of sense," "sentence-sound," "tone," and "intonation."[50] He carefully distinguished between grammar, meaning, meter, and "the sound of sense," which he considered not only "the abstract vitality of our speech," but also "the raw material of poetry," such that "if one is to be a poet he must learn to get cadences by skillfully breaking the sounds of sense with all their irregularity of accent across the regular beat of the metre."[51] Although he regarded "sentence-sounds" as "very definite entities [which] are gathered by the ear from the vernacular," their basis is not cultural or social but biological, since they are innate in the species:

a certain number of sentences (sentence sounds) belong to the human throat just as a certain fixed number of vocal runs belong to the throat of a given kind of bird. These are fixed I say. Imagination cannot create them. It can only call them up. It can only call them up for those who write with their ear on the speaking voice.[52]

Frost asserted at one point that "this is no literary mysticism I am preaching," but he clearly gave his poetics a metaphysical foundation by resorting to biologism, imagining that a set of "fixed" biological properties governs a cultural practice like language use which therefore transcends other, contingent determinations.[53] Ultimately, the poet who attends to "sentence sounds" does undergo a mystical experience: "We summon them from Heaven knows where," Frost wrote, "under excitement with the audile imagination."[54]

Although Frost's examples of "the sound of sense" amounted to English speech rhythms, he occasionally glanced at foreign languages and addressed the question of translating foreign poetry. In a 1915 interview, for example, he used his vernacular poetics to explain the impossibility of translation:

Nobody today knows how to read Homer and Virgil perfectly, because the people who spoke Homer's Greek and Virgil's Latin are dead as the sound of their language. On the other hand, to further emphasize the impossibility of words rather than sound conveying the sense of meaning, take the matter of translation. Really to understand and catch all that is embodied in a foreign masterpiece it must be read in the original because while the words may be brought over the tone cannot be.[55]

Frost's phonocentrism caused him to impose his own poetics on classical poetry, to presume that, like him, Homer and Virgil drew on "sentence sounds" in their writing, thereby erasing its cultural and historical differences. As a result, he believed that when classical poetry is interpreted or translated, as one deferential commentator observed, "we lose the poems because we have lost the sounds."[56] Frost was willing to admit that readers conversant in modern languages could appreciate the "sentence-sounds" of modern-language poetries precisely because they had heard the languages spoken (again presuming that his vernacular poetics was universally valued and implemented). Yet not even those poetries can be translated without omitting the formal feature that makes them poetry: "the words may be brought over," a metaphorical expression by which Frost seems to indicate that the lexical "meaning" of the source text may be communicated in the translating language, but not "the tone" because, presumably, a different language is characterized by a different "sound of sense."

Thus the statement, "poetry is what is lost in translation," requires the assumption of an instrumental model that paradoxically allows Frost to deny the possibility of translation altogether. He conceived of a literary text as a container of invariants, whether formal, semantic, or effective, which a reader can perceive without interpretation. As Untermeyer reports Frost saying in their conversation, a "poem means just what it says and it says what it means, nothing less but nothing more."[57] The invariant that defines a poem is prosodic, sound that nuances meaning, but this formal feature is unavailable to writers and readers who do not speak the language of the poem, and it can never be translated. Without "sentence sounds," Frost asserted, "we can only write the dreary kind of grammatical prose known as professorial [which] is to be seen at its worst in translations especially from the classics."[58]

Frost's instrumentalism prevented him from perceiving aspects of his vernacular poetics that would have challenged his understanding of translation. A classicist, for example, can choose to translate a poem from a classical language into rhythmic prose that cultivates the vernacular, so that the translation avoids a "dreary kind of grammatical prose." But since, in Frost's view, "sentence sounds" are source-text invariants that a translation should but cannot reproduce or transfer, he was unable to imagine that a translator might command a repertoire of discursive strategies, each giving a different nuance to the source text. Frost's instrumentalism, in other words, preempted his thinking of translation as an interpretive act which produces a text in the translating language that is relatively autonomous from the source text, even when the translator is an academic specialist in the source language and can therefore maintain a fairly strict semantic correspondence. This point is demonstrated by the only translation that Frost seems ever to have praised: George Herbert Palmer's 1884 version of *The Odyssey*, which was written in "rhythmic prose."[59]

In 1934, at the invitation of the editor Edward Weeks, Frost sent a list of ten books to be included in a volume called *Books We Like* (1936). His first choice was a translation:

> *The Odyssey* chooses itself, the first in time and rank of all romances. Palmer's translation is by all odds the best. As Lawrence in a preface to his own translation describes the author of the original, he is evidently a man much more like Palmer than like Lawrence. I can permit myself but one translation out of ten books.[60]

Frost was referring to T. E. Lawrence's 1932 version of the Homeric epic, which was similarly translated into prose (and published under the byline of "T. E. Shaw"). In his preface Lawrence remarked that he "tried to deduce the author from his self-betrayal in the work," and on the basis of this Romantic concept of poetry as authorial self-expression, he concluded that Homer was "very bookish, this house-bred man. His work smells of the literary coterie, of a writing tradition."[61] Frost not only agreed with Lawrence's deduction of Homer's personality, but he also knew Palmer personally, having studied with him at Harvard between 1897 and 1899 when Palmer taught there as professor of philosophy. Frost's judgment of Palmer's translation, then, seems to be wholly based on the idea that the sensibilities of both translator and source author were "bookish," and this correspondence resulted in "the best" version.

For any reader familiar with Palmer's project, however, Frost appears to have made a strange lapse. Not only did Palmer assume a hermeneutic model of translation instead of Frost's instrumentalism, but their ideas of Homer were quite different. Palmer asserted in his preface that *The Odyssey* "has as many aspects as it has translators," acknowledging that the Greek text is capable of supporting multiple interpretations, but that none of them can give it back intact since the translator's "sympathies are sure to reach a limit somewhere short of the compass of Homer."[62] Palmer insisted, therefore, that "each translator should distinctly state why the poem has attracted him, so that his readers may better understand what elements may, under his treatment, have been forced into undue prominence."[63] He believed that the interpretation inscribed by a translation is partial, both incomplete in communicating the source text and slanted toward what the translator finds intelligible and interesting, factors that straddle a knowledge of the source text and culture, on the one hand, and an immersion in the translating language and culture, on the other.

And so Palmer explained how he transformed the Greek text:

That which I enjoy most in Homer is his peculiar psychology, his unique ethical attitude; notwithstanding his extraordinary powers of observation and of utterance, he seems to me to confront the world like a child. I turn to him, and escape from our complicated and introspective world, and am refreshed. Accordingly, I have sought to draw attention chiefly to his simplicity, his realism, his finding joy where a child finds it; to his lack of self-consciousness, his interest in a thing or fact for no more ulterior reason than because it is a thing or fact.[64]

Palmer's interpretation prompted him to distinguish Homer from other epic poets, explicitly mentioning Virgil and Milton, who, he observed, "were confessedly bookish men" possessing a "more highly developed mental condition."[65] To maintain this distinction, he chose "to imitate" stylistic features of the Greek text "which characterize the speech of an eager, healthy, sensitive child," including "a syntax full of beauty when thought of as that of living speech."[66] Accordingly, Palmer preferred to use "you" instead of "thou," except for "prayers and solemn occasions," because he favored "the diction of speech instead of that of books."[67]

How, one wonders, could Frost have viewed Palmer's translation as the expression of a "bookish" Homer when the translator deliberately sought to inscribe an interpretation that was opposed to literary sophistication? Frost seems never to have commented on the striking resemblance between his vernacular poetics and Palmer's account of his translation method. The poet obviously felt that his former teacher's version did not contain much "living speech"—which made it worthy of praise. Frost had adopted T. E. Lawrence's competing account of the Homeric text and decided that it corresponded to Palmer's version. In this case, apparently, Frost's investment in instrumentalism was so deep as to suppress the possibility of any distinction between the Greek text, a commentary, and a translation.

Derrida's Paradox

I have analyzed varied uses of two proverbs that continue to receive countless citations—"traduttore traditore" and "poetry is what is lost in translation"—by exploring how their assumption of particular models generates theoretical concepts and discursive practices that derail thinking about translation. The instrumental model that conceives of translation as the reproduction or transfer of a source-text invariant decisively controls the texts where the proverbs originated and have subsequently been used. Because this model privileges certain interpretations to the exclusion of others, it has provoked suspicion about the linguistic competence of translators. More problematic is the fact that instrumentalism gives rise to notions of untranslatability that are linked to metaphysical concepts of textual production and reception. Du Bellay's remarks about the "genius" of a poem and Frost's poetics of "sentence sounds" have proven to be influential examples. Often instrumentalism discloses the possibility of a hermeneutic model which considers translation as an interpretive act that varies the source text according to intelligibilities and interests in the receiving culture. But this competing model is suppressed, at times explicitly through the disparagement of commentary altogether (Franco) or approval of a particular commentator (Nims), at other times tacitly through the mention of a specific concept of equivalence or discursive strategy (du Bellay, Jakobson). The varied uses of the proverbs show that no necessary connection exists between a model of translation and a translation strategy. Instrumentalism can coincide with a strategy that departs from the lexical and syntactical features of the source text (Carew) while a hermeneutic understanding of translation can be put into practice through close adherence to those textual features (Palmer).

Steiner's belief, then, that for millennia translation theory and commentary have shown a paucity of ideas does not quite hold true. Even translation proverbs, despite repeated citation, reveal conceptual differences when their use in specific contexts is taken into account. A certain consistency exists at a more fundamental level, the epistemic level, but here the model underlying a theoretical statement may be aporetic or exposed to contradiction. The assertion that a source text is untranslatable or that translation is generally impossible often presupposes an instrumental model that enables translation to be treated as always unsuccessful. Untranslatability, in other words, depends on the failure of translation understood in a particular way, making a theory of translation necessary to assert that translation is impossible. A particular theoretical statement, furthermore, may be governed by one of the two models, as with the proverbs I have examined, or it may rest on both simultaneously, as with Jakobson's essay, so that comments about concepts and practices of translation divulge a contradiction or logical discontinuity at the epistemic level.

To develop this point further, I want to consider Derrida's paradox—"Rein n'est intraduisible en un sens, mais *en un autre sens* tout est intraduisible" ("In a sense, nothing is untranslatable; but *in another sense* everything is untranslatable")—perhaps the most sophisticated statement to assume the guise of a translation proverb in recent years. In one form or another, whether in French or in English, this statement receives tens of thousands of hits on the internet, mostly in academic publications and scholarly blogs, to be sure, showing that scholarship too may not be immune to cliché. Perhaps the most frequently cited instance, apart from Derrida's own work, is Emily Apter's study, *The Translation Zone* (2006), where each half of the statement provides the title of a different chapter, but neither chapter, nor any another part of the book, actually considers what Derrida may have meant by the paradox, apparently treating it as self-explanatory.[68] This lacuna is symptomatic: Derrida's statement has achieved proverbial status and can now foster rote thinking about translation in the academy.

Although comments about translation appeared early in Derrida's writing, as far back as the 1960s, it was not until some thirty years later that he began to give the paradox a formulaic quality, specifically in two texts: *Le monolinguisme de l'autre* (1996) and "Qu'est-ce qu'une traduction 'relevante'?" (1999). In both cases, the statement is embedded in an exposition that reduces each half to an abstract meaning, exposing their metaphorical status while turning them into vehicles for three different tenors: first, a translation strategy and a paratext, then a concept of equivalence, and finally a notion of untranslatability. Derrida initially suggests that "on peut tout traduire, mais dans une traduction lâche au sens lâche du mot 'traduction'," although the English translator, Patrick Mensah, gives a version that reverts to the passive voice, omitting the pronoun that signifies agency ("on," which might be rendered as "one" or "you" or even "a translator") and edging the English closer to the terse form of a proverb: "everything can be translated, but in a loose translation, in the loose sense of the word 'translation'."[69] Derrida later explains what a "lâche" or "loose" translation might mean by imagining a strategy that includes but exceeds interlingual translation:

> if to a translator who is fully competent in at least two languages and two cultures, two cultural memories with the sociohistorical knowledge embodied in them, you give all the time in the world, as well as the words needed to explicate, clarify, and teach the semantic content and forms of the text to be translated, there is no reason for him to encounter the untranslatable or a remainder in his work.[70]

What Derrida has in mind by "the words needed" is not only translation with latitude, departing from a word-for-word equivalence, but also the addition of paratextual elements like "translator's notes," which mix translation with commentary. Yet "this operation," he points out, "is not what is called a translation," since today translation adheres to "a principle of economy" as a practice

> that, while rendering the so-called proper meaning of a word, its literal meaning (which is to say a meaning that is

determinable and not figural), establishes as the law or ideal—even if it remains inaccessible—a kind of translating that is not *word-to-word*, certainly, or *word-for-word*, but nonetheless stays as close as possible to the equivalence of "one word *by* one word" and thereby respects verbal quantity as a quantity of words, each of which is an irreducible body, the indivisible unity of an acoustic form incorporating or signifying the indivisible unity of a meaning or concept.[71]

Derrida remarks that "this economic equivalence" is "strictly impossible."[72] As a result, each half of the proverb ultimately devolves into a notion of untranslatability: on the one hand, loose translation is not simply translation but also includes commentary which is added because mere translation fails; on the other hand, translation that construes the meaning of the source text according to the unit of the word ends in failure.

The most extraordinary aspect of Derrida's paradox, however, lies in the fact that, regardless of the discourse he introduces to explain it, whether he cites the essentialism of the word in the translation commentary of Cicero and Jerome or the deconstruction of the word in his own poststructuralist thinking, that paradox assumes an instrumental model of translation. This point becomes clear in Derrida's references to translation "without any remainder" ("sans reste").[73] The "remainder" refers to source-text features that are not translated or, for some reason, are not translatable, and so it implicitly treats the source text as a container of invariants which translation should but cannot reproduce or transfer. When Derrida explains that the economic equivalence takes the word as "an irreducible body" where signifier and signified are each an "indivisible unity," he finds this equivalence impossible because of what he elsewhere calls *différance*, the play of differences along a potentially endless chain of signifiers—polysemous, intertextual, subject to infinite linkages—where meaning is always differential and deferred, always already a site of proliferating possibilities.[74] Yet when he suggests that "whenever several words occur in one or the same acoustic or graphic form, whenever a *homophonic* or *homonymic effect* occurs, translation in the strict, traditional and dominant sense of the term encounters an insurmountable limit," an instrumental model comes into play: from the perspective of translation, the originary differential plurality in language constitutes an invariant that cannot be reproduced or transferred.[75] The same point can be made of Derrida's assertion that "a given 'formal' quantity always fails to restore the singular event of the original": the "event" in all its irreducible singularity, when facing the process of translation conceived as economic equivalence, has effectively been turned into an invariant.[76] Derrida's paradox, like other proverbial statements that claim the impossibility of translation, remains within the conceptual parameters of instrumentalism.

Yet on one occasion Derrida does gesture toward a rather different model of translation. In the lecture where he interprets Shakespeare's *The Merchant of Venice* according to the code of translation, arguing that Portia translates Shylock's Judaic discourse of "justice" into the "merciful" discourse that underwrites the "Christian State," he proposes a French version of her line, "when mercy seasons justice."[77] He notes that his version "will not respond to the name *translation*" defined as "that which presents itself as the transfer of an intact signified through the inconsequential vehicle of any signifier whatsoever," and thus he implicitly announces his abandonment of the instrumental model.[78] His translation, furthermore, displays a resourcefulness that can properly be called interpretive in its focus on the key word, "seasons":

Je tradurai donc *seasons* par "relève": "*when mercy seasons justice*", "quand le pardon relève la justice (ou le droit)".

I shall therefore translate "seasons" as "relève": "when mercy seasons justice," "quand le pardon relève la justice (ou le droit)" [*when mercy elevates and interiorizes, thereby preserving and negating, justice (or the law)*].[79]

Derrida translates "seasons" with "relève," the French word he had used three decades before to translate "Aufhebung," Hegel's term for the dialectic, or what Derrida describes as "the double motif of the elevation and the replacement that preserves what it denies or destroys, preserving what it causes to disappear."[80] In my English version of Derrida's lecture, I tried to indicate the conceptual density he assigns to "relève" by inserting within brackets an expansive rendering that incorporates his Hegelian intertext. His choice shows him applying what I would describe as a set of interpretants, two of which are worth specifying here because of their importance to his particular translation: one interpretant is formal or structural, the economic equivalence established by rendering one word by one word, whereas the other is thematic or semantic, his distinctive understanding of the Hegelian dialectic. Translating Portia's line into French requires Derrida's application of these two interpretants, at the very least, whereby he has in effect replaced the instrumentalism of his paradox with a hermeneutic model in which translation inscribes an interpretation in the source text even while maintaining a semantic correspondence (which he explains in considerable detail) that takes the word as the unit of translation.

Derrida's reluctance to label what he has done a translation, along with his remark that it is "without adequation or transparency" in relation to the English source, demonstrates that he was acutely aware of departing from the instrumentalism that continues to dominate contemporary thinking about translation.[81] He regards his version as "assuming the shape of a new writing or rewriting that is performative or poetic."[82] The interpretation inscribed by his translation is performative in the strong, Austinian sense of doing or being (and displacing) Portia's line for Francophones, while it might be considered poetic in the sense that it functions as a figure or trope, constructing an analogy to Derrida's commentary on Hegel's philosophy. The hermeneutics at stake here is interrogative, as we might expect of Derrida, and its impact occurs in three languages: English, German, and French. Rendering "seasons" with "relève" questions, first, the assimilative force in Portia's own translation of Shylock's demands for justice into the Christian discourse of mercy, a translation that entails the Jew's total expropriation and forced conversion to Christianity. But the rendering also points to the Christian metaphysics underlying Hegel's "Aufhebung," where "the movement toward philosophy and absolute knowledge as the truth of the Christian religion passes through the experience of mercy."[83] Finally, Derrida's recourse to "relève" challenges François-Victor Hugo's choice of "tempère" to translate "seasons" in his nineteenth-century version of *The Merchant of Venice*, a choice that is not "erroneous" or "bad," as Derrida observes, but that amounts to a weak interpretation which falls short of questioning the Christians' treatment of Shylock.[84]

We have moved beyond Derrida's lecture in making explicit the assumptions and effects of his experimental translation. In a rapid conclusion, he installs the Hegelian dialectic as "the economy of every interlinguistic translation, this time in the strict and pure sense of the word," insisting on the "Christian dimension" of that dialectic, which can now be recognized as instrumentalist in its application to translation.[85] But Derrida has ignored or set aside the theoretical concepts and practical strategies that might be generated by the hermeneutic model underlying his own innovative practice. We are just beginning to realize how productive this line of inquiry might prove to be—if we question the conventional wisdom enshrined in translation proverbs. Including Derrida's paradox.

3

The Trouble with Subtitles

Instrumentalism in Current Research and Training

Over the past three decades audiovisual translation has emerged as a distinct academic field such that the literature on subtitling has grown into a flood of journal articles and research monographs, edited volumes and conference proceedings, instruction manuals and bibliographies, dissertations and theses.[1] The exponential increase in research has coincided with the worldwide proliferation of programs and courses in academic institutions and professional associations which offer instruction in subtitling and in many cases draw their staff from subtitlers with extensive experience in the film and television industries. Nonetheless, the fundamental theory of translation in most of this research and training, whether that theory is presupposed or formulated explicitly, has remained remarkably unchanged. Repeated emphasis on the "transfer" or "representation" of meaning points to the assumption of the instrumental model of translation.

In a 2011 study Jan Pedersen asserts that "interlingual subtitling is unique in that the message is not only transferred from one language to another, but also from one mode to another: from the spoken mode (usually) to the written mode."[2] Christine Sponholz's 2003 undergraduate thesis at Johannes Gutenberg-Universität Mainz likewise asserts at the outset that "interlingual subtitles transfer the meaning of utterances," and in her survey of translation programs at Western European universities, first among the "special skills" that faculty want students to acquire is "the ability to select and condense the essence of a message."[3] In a 1991 conference paper Henrik Gottlieb, who worked as a subtitler in Danish television for a decade before becoming a university-based scholar-teacher in the field, admits that "often subtitles are indeed less than a true representation of the original message," but he asserts all the same that "a conscientious and talented subtitler is able to operate with a minimal loss of information."[4]

Such statements rest on the instrumental model of translation insofar as the subtitle is assumed to reproduce an invariant contained in or caused by the different language spoken on a film soundtrack, an invariant that is primarily semantic, described as a "message," "meaning," or "information," but that may also be formal or effective. Hence in a 1998 encyclopedia entry on subtitling Gottlieb asserts that "intentions and effects are more important than isolated lexical elements," but he does not consider how this devaluation of the word, phrase, or sentence as the unit of translation might affect the communication of meaning.[5] Instead he implicitly treats meaning as an unchanging essence embedded in the dialogue or the voice-over on the soundtrack, and the subtitle is believed to reproduce that essence in whole or in sufficient part that any "loss" is inconsequential. When the notion of loss is invoked in this instrumental approach to subtitling, it is not associated with any theoretical argument for untranslatability. Just the opposite: it is rather underpinned by an essentialist concept of language that facilitates translation, making it seemingly unproblematic.

More remarkable still is Gottlieb's statement that the "pragmatic dimension" of speech acts "leaves the subtitler free to take certain linguistic liberties" because the medium imposes material constraints that are temporal as well as spatial: the brief period of time allotted to the viewer for reading a subtitle, usually several seconds, and the restriction—for most languages in subtitling cultures—to two lines at the bottom of the frame, each consisting of no more than roughly forty keystrokes that include both characters and spaces.[6] The "liberties" involve condensation of the spoken language or what Gottlieb terms "a quantitative dialogue reduction."[7] Pedersen cites statistics to suggest that "the quantitative condensation rate may average a third" of the dialogue in a film, but this relatively high rate does not lead him to question whether a subtitle does in fact reproduce a semantic invariant: in his view, "Gottlieb has shown that there is not a qualitative loss of information of the same amount. Instead, what is condensed is spoken language features, such as repetitions and false starts," and besides, "viewers are compensated through other channels"—which are audiovisual—"so the total loss of information is not as dire as the quantitative figures suggest."[8] On the contrary, argues Gottlieb, "even deliberate speech, including script-based narration, may contain so much redundancy that a slight condensation will enhance rather than impair the effectiveness of the intended message."[9]

In positing an essential meaning in the soundtrack, the instrumental model at the same time guarantees that the meaning remains intact even after a substantial portion of the soundtrack is omitted from the subtitles. The "intended message" would seem to be immediately available for reproduction; the quantitative reduction is not said to involve any interpretation which can significantly vary that message or which can itself vary according to the interpreter's methods, projected audience, or cultural situation. When audience is considered as a factor in formulating subtitles, it is treated generically as an expenditure of cognitive processing effort, a quantity that is assumed to be uniform for all viewers of the subtitled film and self-evident to the translator. In a subtitling manual that has received wide circulation over the past decade, Jorge Díaz-Cintas and Aline Remael rely on relevance theory from the linguistic field of pragmatics to observe that "it is the balance between the effort required by the viewer to process an item and its relevance for the understanding of the film narrative that determines whether or not it is to be included in the translation."[10] Yet the subtitler can decide this "relevance" only by performing a rather aggressive interpretation so as to isolate not just what the meaning might be but also what might impair it and therefore what necessitates condensation or omission.

I aim to question the prevalent account of subtitling. It lacks the theoretical sophistication that would enable a searching critique of its own thinking as well as the translation practices to which it gives rise. Consequently, it produces sheer mystification instead of illuminating subtitles in a way that is comprehensive and incisive. The main problem is the instrumentalism on which the account rests: this model of translation must be abandoned if the study, teaching, and practice of subtitling are to advance.

Subtitling as Interpretation

The inadequacy of the widely accepted accounts becomes evident in any close examination of a subtitle where a condensation or reduction occurs. In Alfred Hitchcock's film, *Psycho* (1960), for example, secretary Marion Crane buys a used car to make her getaway after stealing $40,000 from her employer. Just after she enters the car lot, she buys and leafs through a newspaper so that she fails to notice that a policeman who had previously questioned her parks his patrol car across the street to observe her movements. Since she is on the run, the sequence of shots creates suspense in the narrative, especially in conjunction with Bernard Herrmann's atmospheric score, a series of modulated crescendos. As Crane rushes to close the deal with the snide car salesman, a point-of-view shot of the policeman watching her insinuates her fear of being arrested, visible in her facial expression. It is during this point-of-view shot that the salesman remarks off-screen: "One thing people never oughta be when they're buyin' used cars and that's in a hurry."[11]

A DVD version of the film that contains subtitles in Italian, French, and German reduces the word count of this English remark to fit within the conventional space constraints, so that each line of the subtitles varies between twenty-three and thirty-nine keystrokes:

Non si dovrebbe mai andare di fretta
quando si compra una macchina.

[One should never be in a hurry
when one buys a car.]

On ne devrait pas être pressé
quand on achète une voiture d'occasion.

[One should not be hurried
when one buys a used car.]

Beim Gebrauchtwagenkauf
sollte man es nie eilig haben.

[When buying a used car
one should never be in a hurry.][12]

In rearranging the clauses, the Italian and French translators have brought the syntax of the subtitles into conformity with the standard dialect of their languages. The German translator also followed the normative word order of German yet rearranged the clauses differently to imitate, at least partially, the sequence of ideas in the salesman's remark—where the syntax is not normative (more on this point below). In each case, the rearrangement was apparently designed to "enhance readability" by applying the principle that "the simpler and more commonly used the syntactic structure of a subtitle, the least effort needed to decipher its meaning"—as one commentator explains these translations.[13] Yet such a purely functional explanation assumes a mechanical adherence to current subtitling conventions, so that it remains superficial in its understanding of the impact of the subtitling. As Díaz-Cintas and Remael observe, "most subtitles display a preference for conventional, neutral word order, and simple well-formed stereotypical sentences."[14] A more incisive explanation would address how the translators' decisions affect the nature of the dialogue, its linguistic and rhetorical dimensions, its role in constructing point of view and characterization, its development of theme, its relation to audiovisual elements like tone of voice and mise-en-scène, and ultimately how these features interact to point to an overall audiovisual effect that solicits the viewer's interpretation of the scene. How, we might more precisely ask, do the translators' verbal choices contribute to the inscription of an interpretation that might exclude other interpretive possibilities?

The subtitles clearly maintain a semantic correspondence according to dictionary definitions for several key words in the English line. Yet more can be said about their lexical and syntactical features and their influence on tone and characterization. Not only are they cast in the standard dialects of Italian, French, and German, but they resort to impersonal constructions: "non si dovrebbe mai" ("one should never"), "on ne devrait pas" ("one should not"), and "sollte man . . . nie" ("one should never"). The tone, as a result, is somewhat formal, so that in these three versions the salesman appears to be politely helpful in providing his customer with advice. Perhaps the Italian version is even more helpful, urging caution when buying any car whatsoever by omitting a translation for the word "used."

The English line, however, can support another, very different interpretation. The salesman's language contains many non-standard items that are markedly colloquial—in pronunciation (the dropping of the "g" in "buying" and the contractions of "ought to," "they are," and "that is"), in lexicon (the generalized use of "people"), and in syntax (the omission of the connective word "that" in the construction "One thing people" and the anacoluthon near the end, where the sentence undergoes a syntactical shift at the word "and"). The register of the English is much lower than that of the Italian, French, and German, and so the salesman, who had initially distinguished himself as voluble and condescendingly sexist ("do anything you've a mind to," he tells Crane, "being a woman you will"), now comes off as fast-talking and sarcastic, even suspicious of Crane's attempt to rush the deal. An Italian, French, or German subtitle could conceivably inscribe this interpretation—and still fit within the conventional space constraints—by varying the use of the standard dialect with an address that is more direct and conversational even if it relies on the polite form for "you" in each language: "Lei non dovrebbe mai"; "Vous ne devriez pas"; "sollte Sie . . . nie." An Italian, French, or German subtitler who perceives the low register of the English might even revert to the familiar form for the pronoun, producing a noticeably colloquial version: "Tu non dovresti mai"; "Tu ne devrais pas"; "solltest du . . . nie."

To be perfectly clear, I am not arguing that my reading of this particular audiovisual image of the salesman is right, nor that the conversational or colloquial subtitles I have suggested as possibilities are correct or accurate. Your agreement with my reading or with the idea of devising a conversational or colloquial subtitle does not make them right or accurate; it just means that I have been persuasive, an effect, at this point in my argument, that is primarily rhetorical even if I have based my reading on linguistic features of the subtitle in relation to audiovisual images. The fact is that the audiovisual image can support at least two, possibly three interpretations that strain logic, if they are not mutually exclusive: the salesman as politely helpful or as sarcastically suspicious or both at once. And each interpretation can lead to a particular translation of the spoken line that implements certain verbal choices but not others. The viewer's decision as to how the subtitle should be interpreted, moreover, can ensure a corroborating interpretation of the audiovisual image, of the montage and the actor's voice, or, vice versa, the viewer's interpretation of the image can ensure the selection of a particular interpretation of the subtitle. The absence of the car salesman from the shot when he speaks the line exacerbates the indeterminacy I am describing.

The soundtrack, in other words, is not available in some unmediated form or in a form that is free of the nuances introduced by the audiovisual image and by a subtitle, if one is present. Any comment on the soundtrack therefore is already an interpretation that works to synthesize audiovisual elements. I have transcribed the car salesman's line with an orthography that stresses not only the colloquialism of his language, its sheer orality, but also the informality, indeed the familiarity of his manner toward Marion Crane. Even my back translations of the Italian, French, and German subtitles into English should be seen as interpretations, since the English versions fix a meaning by highlighting different pronominal forms in each language, whether impersonal, formal/polite, or informal/familiar.

No interpretation, furthermore, can be privileged merely on the strength of a comparison to the soundtrack because the interpretation would need to establish a basis or criterion for that comparison by fixing the form, meaning, or effect of specific speech acts as well as visual images—and that fixing is itself an interpretive act. A conversational or colloquial subtitle in Italian, French, or German, then, cannot be taken as necessarily more adequate to the English line: it would depend on a prior interpretation that fixes the English as conversational or colloquial, establishing a different network of intertextual and interdiscursive connections for Italian, French, and German viewers and soliciting a different mode of reception from the one that greeted the soundtrack in Anglophone cultures. For any departure from the standard dialect of those translating languages, especially a departure from impersonal or formal/polite forms, would be noticeable to viewers since it would mean a deviation from linguistic and social conventions that apply when a salesman deals with a potential customer in a transaction like buying a car. For some viewers, to use a familiar form of "you" in Italian, French, or German could characterize the salesman as forward to the point of impolite, even confrontational, no longer simply helpful.

The subtitles show that every translation entails shifting between source and receiving contexts. Translating detaches the source text from a complicated originary context (intratextual, intertextual, interdiscursive, intersemiotic or intermedial) by dismantling, rearranging, and displacing features that are constitutive of that text insofar as they support meanings, values, and functions in the source culture. At the same time, translating builds a different but equally complicated context for the source text such that it can no longer be called merely "the source text": it is rewritten in the translating language and comes to possess different constitutive features that can support different meanings, values, and functions in the receiving culture.

The instrumental model of translation that underlies so much subtitling research, teaching, and practice fails to consider these factors, and so it cannot analyze the connections between verbal choices and interpretive moves. In fact, it does not even recognize the existence of such connections or the range of interpretive possibilities open to subtitlers. To explore those possibilities, we need to adopt a hermeneutic model in which translation is seen as an interpretive act that varies the form, meaning, and effect of the source material according to the conditions—linguistic, cultural, and social—that the translator selects to frame the interpretation. These conditions, which come from both the source and receiving cultures, are formal and thematic interpretants that mediate between the source material and the translation—a specific structure of equivalence, for example, or a particular interpretation of the audiovisual image. Only a hermeneutic model of translation, as I have been arguing throughout this book, can expose the manifold conditions of any translation and avoid the mystification entailed by instrumentalism. A hermeneutic model takes for granted that translation is transformation, even when a semantic correspondence is strictly maintained or a stylistic approximation is established. And it seeks to take responsibility for that transformation not only by providing a transparent account of the interpretation inscribed in the source material but also by considering the impact of the inscription in the cultural situations where the translation is produced and received.

The advance made possible by the hermeneutic model becomes more evident if we use it to examine the difficult problems posed by translating culture-specific items or, in Pedersen's terminology, "extralinguistic cultural references." He defines such references as

attempted by means of any cultural linguistic expression, which refers to an extralinguistic entity or process. The referent of the said expression may prototypically be assumed to be identifiable to a relevant audience as this referent is within the encyclopaedic knowledge of this audience.[15]

Pedersen provides an example from Larry Gelbart and Gene Reynolds's television series, M*A*S*H, which was not only long-running in the United States (1972–1983) but widely viewed abroad. In one episode, the deranged intelligence officer Colonel Sam Flagg explains how he taught himself not to laugh or smile: "I watched a hundred hours of the Three Stooges. Every time I felt like smiling, I jabbed myself in the stomach with a cattle prod."[16] Pedersen observes that the reference to the Three Stooges would be "obscure to Scandinavian audiences," so the Danish subtitler replaced it with another, "accessible" reference by inserting a phrase that came to be a conventional translation of "Laurel and Hardy" into Danish, "Gøg og Gokke":

Jeg så Gøg og Gokke film i 100 timer.

I watched Laurel and Hardy movies for 100 hours.[17]

Pedersen remarks that some Danish viewers might notice the discrepancy between the English line spoken on the soundtrack and the Danish subtitle, although he limits their possible responses to the unconsidered judgment that the translation is erroneous.

Pedersen argues, however, that the choice is not an error but "a highly felicitous solution" that actually establishes an equivalence to the English. "The subtitler," he asserts, "has sought equivalence of effect, rather than equivalence of information."[18] Pedersen explains this distinction by citing the translation theorist Eugene Nida's notion of "dynamic equivalence," which is based on what Nida calls "the principle of equivalent effect." In Nida's words,

> In such a translation, one is not so concerned with matching the receptor-language message with the source-language

message, but with the dynamic relationship, that the relationship between receptor and message should be substantially the same as that which existed between the original receptors and the message.[19]

Pedersen, like Nida before him, is assuming the instrumental model of translation: the equivalent effect is understood to be an invariant caused by the source text—in this case, the comical effect of the cultural reference in the dialogue—and the subtitle is thought to reproduce or transfer that effect without change. Pedersen can make this assumption, however, only by ignoring various complicating factors. Laurel and Hardy have in fact been substituted for the Three Stooges, introducing a significant difference. Some segments of the Danish audience may understand English and detect the discrepancy. And different audience segments, whether in Denmark or in Anglophone countries, are likely to have quite different responses to the two comedy teams.

These factors indicate beyond a doubt that the notion of equivalent effect is a naïve fiction. Because translating entails shifting between source and receiving contexts, no translation can elicit a response from its reader that is the same as or closely similar to the response elicited from the source-language reader by the source text—even if we set aside the problem that readerships are heterogeneous cultural constituencies, so that describing any response to the source text requires that a segment of source-language readers be specified. In reality, the notion of equivalent effect involves an interpretive act that has generally gone unexamined: it reduces the source material and its translation to a shared meaning that strips away any formal and thematic differences, and it performs this semantic reduction on the basis of the instrumental model in which the meaning is assumed to be invariant, free of the variations that always occur among different cultural constituencies in the same or different social formations at the same or different historical moments. In the example from the Danish version of *M*A*S*H*, this shared meaning might be phrased as "a slapstick comedy team" or, more precisely, broad humor in the form of physical and verbal comedy.

Hence Pedersen's instrumentalism excludes other interpretive possibilities. For the fact remains that the Three Stooges were not Laurel and Hardy, and these two comedy teams performed different routines and received different responses from their audiences, whether those audiences are understood as elite or popular. In the United States, both teams achieved popularity. But the Three Stooges were long marginalized in film studies because their brand of slapstick humor was considered lowbrow, "too vulgar to be taken seriously," whereas Laurel and Hardy were seen as sophisticated and made the object of scholarly atten- tion at least as early as the 1960s.[20] Laurel and Hardy were also very popular in Scandinavia, so much so that their names were assigned a conventional translation in Scandinavian languages, and not only were their films distributed in the region, but in the 1940s they toured there with their act. The Three Stooges' films, as Pedersen puts it, "never made it to Scandinavia."[21]

In view of the international reception of the two comedy teams, the change in reference from "the Three Stooges" to "Gøg og Gokke" cannot be reduced to a simple difference between unintelligibility and an intelligible joke. It affects the charac- terization of Colonel Flagg, first of all, who in English is more buffoonish but in Danish more endearing, even more cultured in his appreciation of classic film comedy, depending on the audience segment who views the episode, on their knowledge of Anglophone film traditions and genres. The use of "Gøg og Gokke," furthermore, domesticates Flagg's line for any Danish audience who recognizes the conventional translation, working to erase the cultural difference of a U.S. television program by assimilating it to a dominant cultural value in Danish, a familiar form of popular culture. If the reference to the Three Stooges had been retained with a close translation into Danish, it would not necessarily have been unintelligible: some viewers could have inferred from the context, from Flagg's mention of "smiling," that it signified a form of film comedy, in fact comedy so funny that the electrical shock of a cattle prod is necessary to suppress laughter. More importantly, the retention of the Three Stooges would have simultaneously registered a sense of foreignness by signifying film comedy that had originated in a different culture but without circulating in Scandinavia. The use of "Gøg og Gokke" blurs the distinction between foreign and domestic, making M*A*S*H seem familiar, even somewhat Danish, and inviting the sort of complacent response that can accompany the recognition of a cultural reference.

Pedersen's notion that such references in a soundtrack are "extralinguistic" must be seen as a questionable reification forced by his instrumentalism. A culture-specific item never exists outside of some form of representation or semiosis, so that it comes to cultural forms and practices laden with significance that has accrued from its circulation through different media, print and electronic, as well as through the different institutions in which such media are housed. It is only the reification produced by an essentialist concept of language that would detach an item from this cultural process, at once complex and cumulative. Translated into "Gøg og Gokke," Laurel and Hardy have been received differently in Denmark than in Anglophone cultures. After all, their films, both silent and sound, were themselves translated, i.e., screened with Danish intertitles and subtitles.

How to Read Subtitles

One might think that subtitlers, adept at dealing with such translation problems as those we have examined, would develop an intuitive sense of the hermeneutic model and come to regard their work as fundamentally an interpretive act that inevitably transforms the source material. But this progression does not seem to have happened much. Regardless of whether they learned subtitling on the job or studied it in a translator training program, their rare accounts of their work remain not only unreflective but uncritical, showing an unwillingness to question current subtitling conventions.

A pertinent example is offered by Henri Béhar, a noted French subtitler who also produces and directs programs for French radio and television. Since 1983 Béhar has subtitled over one hundred French and English films. He contributed an essay to Atom Egoyan and Ian Balfour's edited volume, *Subtitles* (2004), in which he discusses his inventive English subtitles for Alain Cavalier's film, *Thérèse* (1986):

> the young nun who was to become Sainte Thérèse de Lisieux had an unfettered, juvenile passion for Christ, and her "beefs" with Jesus had the flavour of a lovers' quarrel. I decided (with Cavalier's consent) to keep all references to Christ in the lower case ("he" instead of "He," "thine" instead of "Thine," etc.). One American critic who saw the film in an advance preview thought the director was "showing disrespect and reduced the whole dialogue between Thérèse and Jesus to a lovers' tiff."[22]

In making his verbal choices, Béhar assumed a hermeneutic model, although unwittingly. When he writes, "I decided," he implicitly refers to his application of two kinds of interpretants: one is formal, a concept of equivalence that can be defined as a semantic correspondence to the French dialogue, what Béhar calls "trying to make sure you get it all right,"[23] while the other is thematic, his own interpretation of Thérèse's psychological state and religious devotion (her "unfettered, juvenile passion for Christ" expressed as "a lovers' quarrel"). This interpretation led Béhar to create a distinct style, another formal interpretant: it consists of the lower case when Thérèse addresses Christ as well as a mixture of current standard English with nonstandard items which include colloquialisms (as the very word "beefs" suggests) and an early modern form like "thine," evocative of the King James Bible. Béhar clearly treats his verbal choices as interpretive moves even if he never uses the word "interpretation." The fact that he "decided" to make those choices implies that he could have decided otherwise, choosing different language to inscribe a different interpretation of Thérèse's devotion to Christ.

The American critic's disapproval, in contrast, is based on the prevalent instrumentalism. The critic assumes that the director Cavalier deposited a semantic invariant in the screenplay, "a lovers' tiff," which was signified in "the whole dialogue between Thérèse and Jesus" as recorded on the soundtrack and which was subsequently reproduced in the subtitles in an unbroken chain of signification. In this instrumentalist response, Béhar's crucial intervention is rendered invisible: the critic blamed the director, not the subtitler. Béhar could of course have used conventional punctuation, upper case for sacred figures, as well as current standard English throughout. Here too the subtitler's interpretive labor would have been invisible to the critic, but only because the subtitler would have applied the interpretants that the critic finds most acceptable in representing a young nun's address to Christ: strict adherence to linguistic norms resulting in a formal register that shows respect for divinity. The critic's instrumentalism masks rather than discloses his own interpretive act in which religious representation is made to answer to a concept of stylistic decorum so as to produce a specific variety of the realist illusion, a specific notion of what can stand for reality in a film biography of a saint.

What leads film viewers, including critics, to adopt an instrumental model of translation in their response to subtitles? More often than not viewers are likely to assume this model with every kind of translation they encounter, but in the case of film we must figure in their deep investment in what Luis Pérez-González has called the "representational conventions" of the medium: the combination of continuity editing, spatiotemporal coherence, narrative causality, and synchronous sound which creates the diegesis, the fictional world where the characters enact the plot.[24] The construction of this illusory reality is supported by subtitles that provide basic narrative information through condensation, reformulation, and omission, among other conventional strategies of manipulating the speech on the soundtrack.[25] In the viewer's response, the subtitles are effectively subsumed into the diegesis, whereas they are by definition nondiegetic elements, comparable to credits or music, which are added to the narrative. This response rests on the assumption that the subtitles reproduce a semantic invariant contained in the characters' dialogue. As Pérez-González puts it, "in purporting to represent the diegetic reality, audiovisual translation practices convey a PRESUMPTION OF FAITHFULNESS."[26]

Conspicuously missing from Pérez-González's account, however, is any mention of specific linguistic features, even though subtitling is a variety of interlingual translation. These features reveal the instrumentalism that ultimately underlies any uncritical acceptance of the collusion between subtitling and the filmic diegesis. Because the language of translation throughout the world today tends to be extremely homogeneous, regardless of the genre or text type or medium, because it adheres mostly to the current standard dialect and therefore the most familiar and accessible form of the translating language,[27] subtitles written in this language can easily produce the illusion of transparency, giving the impression that they communicate the speech on the soundtrack directly, in an untroubled fashion, while reinforcing the realism of the film through their unobtrusiveness. This discursive regime of transparent translation, along with the representational conventions of film, has fostered the expectation that the subtitler should be invisible.

Béhar's departures from current standard English frustrate that expectation and call attention to themselves—as the American critic's response makes clear. Béhar's subtitles proved to be so subversive of conventional practices that when the English version of Cavalier's film was released, whether as a 35 mm print or on VHS and DVD, the subtitles were revised by another translator, Matthew Pollack, without Béhar's permission or even his knowledge, so that both Béhar and Pollack are credited.[28] As a result, a version of the film with Béhar's original subtitles is virtually impossible to find; his essay presents the only evidence for his translation strategies. Since Béhar did not retain a copy of his subtitles, furthermore, the nature and extent of Pollack's revisions cannot be determined with any exactness: colloquialisms seem to have been retained, but any archaisms were replaced by standard usage.

Yet the most troubling aspect of this case is the lack of comprehension and critical self-awareness that are displayed not so much in the critic's comment as in Béhar's. Despite the inventiveness of his subtitling, Béhar seems to be unable to grasp its theoretical and practical implications. Immediately after describing his work on Cavalier's film, he asserts that

> Subtitling is a form of cultural ventriloquism, and the focus must remain on the puppet, not the puppeteer. Our task as subtitlers is to create subliminal subtitles so in sync with the mood and rhythm of the movie that the audience isn't even aware it is reading. We want *not* to be noticed.[29]

Béhar's subtitling really points in a very different direction. It encourages in the audience not a "subliminal" response, unconscious of his intervention, but an active engagement with the subtitles as texts in their own right, relatively autonomous from the soundtrack insofar as they were created by a translator in a different language for a different culture on the basis of a rather specific interpretation of the source material. In Béhar's view, however, the ideal subtitles are "so in sync with the mood and rhythm of the movie" as to be invisible. Thus he supports the collusion between the translation and the diegesis and implicitly regards his interpretation of the film as true or right, overlooking the possibility that Cavalier's representation of Thérèse's life might be interpreted in varying ways. Béhar's translation practice shows him performing an interpretive act, but his commentary on his practice is resolutely instrumentalist.

The key problem posed by this case, then, is not that viewers are forced to become aware of subtitles like Béhar's (i.e., his original, unrevised version), but rather that viewers do not know how to understand or process them. If viewers assume a hermeneutic model of translation, resisting the complete subsumption of the subtitles into the diegesis, they can perceive Béhar's verbal choices as based on but distinct from the audiovisual images in the French film, constituting an interpretation in English because nonstandard items like colloquialisms and archaisms not only deviate from conventional subtitling practices but also derive from a particular moment in the history of the English language. Understood in this way, the subtitles need not provoke an unpleasurable experience when the viewer becomes aware of them; on the contrary, they can enhance the viewer's appreciation of the film, whether or not that viewer understands the language spoken on the soundtrack.

Another example can serve to demonstrate and develop this point further. It involves a pun which, because it depends on sound, is usually doomed to be omitted in the translation process since the acoustic features of language are the first to be affected. Unless, of course, the translator is so resourceful that he or she manages to devise a comparable pun in the translating language. In this case, what needs to be considered is the semantic load of the pun, the different meanings by which the translation inscribes an interpretation of the film.

The pun I want to consider occurs near the beginning of Woody Allen's film *Annie Hall* (1977), where Alvy Singer manifests his paranoia about anti-Semitism in a conversation with his friend Rob:

ALVY: I distinctly heard it. He muttered under his breath "Jew."
ROB: You're crazy!
ALVY: No, I'm not. We were walking off the tennis court, and you know, he was there and me and his wife, and he looked at her and then they both looked at me, and under his breath he said, "Jew."
ROB: Alvy, you're a total paranoid.
ALVY: Wh—How am I a paran—? Well, I pick up on those kinds o' things. You know, I was having lunch with some guys from NBC, so I said . . . uh, "Did you eat yet or what?" and Tom Christie said, "No, didchoo?" Not, did you, didchoo eat? Jew? No, not did you eat, but jew eat? Jew. You get it? Jew eat?[30]

The play on "didchoo" and "Jew" resists recreation in other languages because it turns on a particular pronunciation of the English phrase, "did you." On the DVD version of the film,[31] the French subtitles make a strained effort to recreate the pun by introducing the irrelevant notion of tiredness ("Je suis fatigué," meaning "I am tired") so as to approximate the sound of "Juif," the French word for "Jew." As Alvy explains to Rob, Tom Christie said, "juif-/atigué au lieu de 'Je suis fatigué.'" The Spanish subtitles make no effort of any kind to imitate the pun. There

Alvy reports Tom Christie's response to his question as a blunt insult: Christie says simply, "No. ¿Y tú, judío?" ("No. And you, Jew?"). The French and Spanish subtitles can be taken in conflicting ways: either they substantiate Alvy's concern about racist remarks or they are so extreme as to be ludicrously untrue, amounting to an absurd exaggeration and therefore serving as evidence of his paranoia.

José Luis Guarner, the Catalan film critic who published a Spanish translation of the screenplay in 1981, created a brilliant pun to replace the English word:

ALVY: Le oí perfectamente. Dijo "judío" en voz baja.

ROB: ¡Tú estás loco!

ALVY: Que no, hombre. Salíamos de la pista de tenis, ¿sabes?, estábamos él, su mujer y yo. La miró, se volvieron los dos hacia mí y él murmuró entre dientes "judío."

ROB: Alvy, eres un paranoico total.

ALVY ¿Qué . . . qué yo soy un parano . . . ? A mí esas cosas no se me escapan, ya lo sabes. Mira, tenía que almorzar con unos tipos de la NBC, y yo pregunté: "¿Habéis comido ya, o qué?", y Tom Christie me respondió: "Sí, judías". No dijo: "Ya hemos comido", sino "Sí, judías". ¡Judías! ¿Te das cuenta? "Sí, judías".[32]

The word, "judías," perfectly fits the context, the lunchtime conversation between Alvy and Tom Christie, because it signifies a food in peninsular Spanish, "green beans." Yet because the word can also signify "Jewish women," a meaning activated by the topic of Alvy's conversation with Rob, it works as a pun and conveys the racist innuendo that Alvy detects. Nonetheless, Guarner's interpretation, although supported by the English dialogue, introduces a difference that transforms the characterization of Alvy: in the English Alvy is truly paranoid in that he hears the word "Jew" when it is not in fact uttered, whereas in the Spanish Tom Christie uses a word that does refer to Jews and can be taken as an anti-Semitic slur, possibly a double entendre, but in any case a reference that justifies Alvy's suspicion and suggests that he is not as paranoid as he may seem. The Spanish pun puts these meanings into play but does not decide among them.

Although for the most part Spain handles audiovisual translation through dubbing (reserving Spanish subtitles for foreign-language films screened in their original versions), Guarner's text can conceivably be turned into subtitles that fit within the conventional space constraints. A Spanish viewer who assumes the instrumental model of translation will merely respond to the Spanish pun as if it reproduced the meaning of Alvy's line on the soundtrack—and probably erupt in laughter. A viewer who assumes the hermeneutic model will laugh too, but this viewer is likely to recognize the subtitler's hand. The recognition would be based on the awareness that the pun is specific to the Spanish of Spain, not Latin America, it can function only in peninsular Spanish, even if it imitates some verbal effect in the English dialogue, and so the subtitler's resourcefulness is deserving of admiration. A more reflective viewer might take another step to interpret the subtitler's interpretation, perceiving how the Spanish pun alters Alvy's characterization from a paranoid schlemiel to the schlemiel who actually suffers an anti-Semitic slur, however comical it may seem in the context of the film. The reflective viewer who can understand English but who is also inclined toward suspicious responses might take yet another step to discern that Guarner's pun interrogates Allen's screenplay: it exposes the fact that the English treats anti-Semitism as a form of paranoia that can become the basis of jokes, even as the English comes back to worry the equivalence of the Spanish version and to point up the pressure to represent an instance of persecution—perhaps not surprising in a translation published within a decade after the end of Franco's fascist dictatorship. The subtitle, in other words, like any translation, can be seen as setting up a critical dialectic with the source material whereby they submit one another to a probing critique—although only when approached with the hermeneutics of suspicion, as Paul Ricoeur called it, discounting the seemingly coherent surface of a text so as to probe for latent meanings through omissions, additions, or discrepancies.[33]

To state what may seem obvious but has so far remained implicit: this sort of response to subtitles, theoretically informed and methodologically sophisticated, must be learned, like any kind of literacy. And what better place to begin the instruction than with subtitlers themselves. If subtitlers explore the range of potential viewer responses by analyzing subtitles produced by their more experimental colleagues, they can be inspired to expand their stylistic repertoires in relation to the interpretive challenges presented by each new film they are commissioned to translate. Unfortunately, the dominant pedagogy for audiovisual translation preempts any such instruction because it remains so deeply instrumentalist—even when the instructor's own research puts into question the notion that a subtitle reproduces an invariant contained in or caused by the soundtrack. A 2009 essay by Christopher Taylor, who has trained translators for many years at the University of Trieste, illustrates the contradictory moves that an instructor might make to preserve the very notion of invariance in translation.

Taylor's piece, "Pedagogical Tools for Training Subtitlers," is framed by two premises of which "subtitlers must be aware" in his view and which he presents as "lessons" for subtitling practice: the first, derived from "communication linguistics," is that "film scripts are 'written to be spoken as if not written,'" while the second is that "subtitles are, in a sense, 'written to be

read as if not written.'"[34] Thus an unbroken chain of signification is imagined between screenplay and subtitle such that the
realist illusion of orality in the screenplay is initially reproduced
in the actors' performances, then in the audiovisual images of
those performances, and finally in the subtitles.

In articulating the two "lessons," however, Taylor raises
serious doubts about the continuity of this signifying chain.
He first describes research "experiments" that involved "comparing the scripts of fifty modern films set in contemporary,
'real' environments with an equivalent-sized sample of spoken
language from the Cobuild Bank of English corpus," noting
that "the film scripts differed considerably from the corpus
sample."[35] Not only does Taylor conclude that the experiments
"point to the difficulty of reproducing genuine oral discourse
in film," but he proceeds to observe that "transcriptions of film
dialogue often show discrepancies in relation to the original
script, as the actors begin to 'feel' the part and, as a result,
render the dialogue more authentic," thereby reinforcing the
illusion of orality that was tenuous in the screenplay.[36] Taylor's faith in this reinforcement actually seems to be rather
weak since, in an effort to include viewer "interpretation"
among his pedagogical tools, he ultimately asserts that "the
words of subtitles represent a distinct (macro) genre and are
not interpreted in the same way as written scripted words,
words on the screen in the original language or the spoken
words."[37] Unfortunately, Taylor explains neither the nature of
the "distinct (macro) genre" that subtitles constitute nor the
mode of interpretation that viewers are generically prompted
to apply to them.

Yet enough of his exposition has been quoted to pose a crucial question: if the illusion of orality in a screenplay tends
to be compromised when the film is made and if viewers do
not interpret subtitles as oral discourse, why should subtitlers

still translate as if their subtitles reproduce the speech on the soundtrack, maintaining an illusion of transparency that can allow their translation to pass for that speech itself? The fact that Taylor does not formulate or address this question indicates that in the end he is unable to abandon the instrumentalism that frames his essay. Despite evidence to the contrary, he clings to the notion that subtitling is the reproduction of an effect, the realism of the dialogue, which he would like to regard as invariant but which film production and reception submit to such continuous variation as to suggest that it exists most forcefully, if at all, in the subtitler's interpretation as inscribed in the subtitles.

Measuring Progress

Given the instrumentalism that dominates subtitling research, teaching, and practice, limiting them to uncritical superficiality, where do we locate the possibility of advancing the field? The film industry has recently witnessed the emergence of new subtitling practices in feature-length films, the area that has been most resistant to change. Although these practices remain peripheral in the industry, they reveal the increasing adoption of a hermeneutic model of translation whereby the subtitler applies formal and thematic interpretants that depart from subtitling conventions.

The departures usually incorporate nonstandard linguistic items, so that the subtitler's interpretation is most likely to become visible to viewers steeped in conventional subtitling which favors the current standard dialect of the translating language. Viewers need not know the source language to notice and develop a certain appreciation of the subtitler's work, even if that appreciation will not involve comparing the translation to the source text. Instead their viewing experience must be critically sophisticated, capable of reading a subtitle in relation to the different aspects of an audiovisual image and of analyzing how the translation might nuance characterization, construct narrative, or evoke genre. To enable this approach, the viewer too must adopt a hermeneutic model, setting out from the assumption that subtitling, like all translation, performs an interpretive act which can establish both a semantic correspondence and a stylistic approximation to the speech on the soundtrack while still transforming that speech according to what is intelligible and interesting in the receiving culture. As we have seen with Henri Béhar, furthermore, even accomplished subtitlers may not intend the kind of visibility I aim to bring to subtitling or be able to provide a theoretically informed account of their work. Subtitles, like any text, can release or support effects that escape the subtitler's conscious control only to be grasped or elaborated by the thoughtful viewer.

The new subtitling is a distinctive feature of the Criterion Collection, the New York City–based distribution company that for more than three decades has been issuing classic and contemporary films in restored versions with supplementary materials like interviews and commentary, first on LaserDisc (1984–1998) and then on DVD (from 1998) and Blu-ray Disc (from 2008). The reissues include hundreds of foreign-language films that have in many cases been resubtitled in English. Hence changes in translation practices can be gauged by comparing the subtitles on a Criterion DVD with a previous version of a film, which may date back to an original 35 mm print that was subsequently released on VHS and DVD.

As an example I have chosen Jules Dassin's film noir of a jewelry shop robbery with a tragic ending, *Du rififi chez les hommes* (1955) or *Rififi*, as it is commonly called.[38] In the series of extracts I present below, the uncredited subtitles from a VHS version released in 1998 (on the left) are juxtaposed to Lenny Borger's subtitles on the Criterion DVD released in 2001 (on the right). Since 1990 Borger, a Brooklyn-born journalist and translator who has long resided in Paris, has written the English subtitles for roughly one hundred French films, including the work of such important directors as Robert Bresson, Luis Buñuel, Marcel Carné, Jean-Luc Godard, Louis Malle, and Jean Renoir. To facilitate the comparative analysis while creating a representative sample, I have divided the subtitles for the opening scene of *Rififi* into four exchanges and inserted a transcription of the French soundtrack for each exchange. The spelling, punctuation, and lineation, as well as the language, duplicate what appears on the screen with one or two lines assigned to a frame.

The first exchange begins right after the credits with a shot of a poker game, at first a close-up of a table strewn with cards and chips. The camera then shows the players, focusing on Tony who has depleted his supply of chips and now folds his hand. As the cards are gathered for another deal, Tony speaks to another player, and the subtitles begin:

TONY: Paulo, prête-moi vingt sacs.
PAUL: Impossible, Tony. Tu sais qu'au jeu . . .
TONY: C'est bon. Je vais m'en faire apporter.

TONY: Lend me twenty Paul	Paulo . . .
	Stake me.
PAUL: Impossible, Tony . . .	Impossible, Tony.
We're playing cards . . .	Not during a game.
TONY: All right, I'll send for it.	Okay.
	I'll call for cash.

Tony leaves the room briefly to phone his friend Jo. In the second exchange, Tony has returned to the back room where the game is being played as another hand is dealt. But he is not given any cards:

TONY: Servez-moi.

PLAYER 2: On ne joue pas sur parole ici.

TONY: Ça vient.

PLAYER 2: Pas de pognon, pas de cartes.

TONY: And me?	How about me?
PLAYER 2: No credit here.	We don't bet promises here.
No dough, no cards.	No cash, no cards.

In the third exchange, Jo enters the room:

JO: C'est moi que t'attends?

TONY: Oui. Tu vois? La confiance règne.

JO: Bon Dieu, vous le connaissez, c'est Tony le Stephanois tout de même.

PAUL: Tony ou pas on s'en fout. Une seule chose compte, le pognon.

JO [TO TONY]: Laisse tomber ces truffes.

JO: Waiting for me?	You waiting for me?
TONY: Confidence reigns supreme!	Yeah. Their faith
	is touching.
JO: You know him!	But you all know him.
It's Tony Stephanois!	He's Tony the Stephanois!
PAUL: Only one thing counts here,	Tony or no Tony,
dough!	only one thing counts . . .
	Hard cash.
JO [TO TONY]: Forget these lice.	Forget these lugs.

In the fourth exchange, immediately following Jo's offensive remark about the other players, the man whom I have identified as "Player 2" rises from the table, walks over to Jo and Tony, who are standing in a corner of the room, and taps Jo on the shoulder:

PLAYER 2: Dis donc. T'es pas poli.

JO: Ça te défrise?

PLAYER 2: Hey you there!   Hey, you!
          You're not very polite.   You're not polite.
JO: Oh you object?   That bug you?

At Jo's last remark, Player 2 is about to reach his right hand into his inside jacket pocket as if for a weapon, but Tony stops him by placing his hand on the player's:

TONY: L'énerve pas, c'est un jeune.
[TO JO] Allez, viens.

TONY: Relax my friend.   Relax. He's still green.
[TO JO] Let's go.   Let's go.

Both sets of subtitles communicate sufficient information to orient the reader to the action as it unfolds, and both begin to sketch the psychological contours of the characters as well as the nature of their shady milieu, potentially dangerous yet informed by particular rules and values that maintain order. All the same, a significant difference emerges: the previous version shows a tendency, even if not entirely consistent, to reduce the soundtrack to the fewest words necessary to understand the exchange, whereas Borger's subtitles offer a fuller, more complete translation. Thus the sentence, "on ne joue pas sur parole ici" (one does not play on talk here), is condensed to "no credit here" in the first set of subtitles, but Borger translates it as "we don't bet promises here," where "promises" specifies the French, "parole" (talk, speech, word). Borger's subtitles are definitely clearer and more precise than the previous version. The meaning of Tony's closely translated remark, "confidence reigns supreme" ("la confiance règne"), is too obscure to be grasped in the seconds that the viewer must read it, whereas Borger's choice of the freer rendering, "their faith is touching," is not only comprehensible but plainly sarcastic in context. The previous version deletes Tony's reference to Jo's inexperience, "c'est un jeune" (he is a young man), but Borger translates it by inserting a sentence, "he's still green," which is clarifying as well, although with a rather different effect: it strengthens the plausibility of the scene by providing Player 2 with a motive not to draw his weapon in retaliation for Jo's insult.

Following the French colloquialism and slang on the soundtrack, both sets of subtitles also resort to nonstandard English in lexicon and syntax. Thus either "dough" or "hard cash" is used for "pognon," which is slang for "money," and the translations each create clipped constructions like "waiting for me?" and "you waiting for me?" for "c'est moi que t'attends?" (is it me that you are expecting?). Still, Borger's use of nonstandard items is more consistent and extensive, so much so as to appear systematic. Where the previous version chooses the standard dialect, "lend me twenty," Borger relies on gambling jargon, "stake me," and he replaces standard items like "lice" and "oh you object?" with slang, "lugs" and "that bug you?"

These examples are typical of Borger's subtitles throughout the film. When Tony, Jo, and their fellow thief Mario discuss the jewelry shop heist, Tony insists that they not carry guns. The previous version casts his rationale in standard syntax with a slang term for a prison sentence, "a gun can get you a stretch for life," whereas Borger relies more heavily on criminal language in nonstandard syntax: "Get caught with a rod, / and it's the slammer for life." In the previous version, similarly, when Tony insists that the robbery needs to be more ambitious, the minimal use of slang combined with the standard dialect seems restrained—

The show-case, the daylight job
kid's stuff.
Let's go for something worthwhile,
The safe!—

especially when compared to Borger's lively evocation of thieves' cant:

> For me, the rocks in the window
> are chicken feed.
> We gotta go for the real thing.
> The jackpot. The safe!

Although the sort of close comparison I have made here would not be attempted by most viewers, film critics have occasionally commented on the subtitles in revealing ways. In 1956, when *Rififi* was first screened in the United States, the film was favorably received, and the subtitles seemed adequate. Bosley Crowther, the critic for the *New York Times* who appears to have understood the French soundtrack, noted that "the dialogue is well translated in English subtitles which say everything except the dirty words."[39] Yet Crowther's reference to the untranslated obscenities along with his idea that the subtitles "say everything" suggests that his criterion for evaluating the translation was not very rigorous: it amounted to little more than the demand for a semantic correspondence that enables the viewer to follow the narrative.

Some four decades later, Lenny Borger felt differently when he was commissioned to resubtitle a restored 35 mm print. In an interview I asked him if he examined previous translations of *Rififi* before beginning his work, and he explained that he had, although he deliberately avoided their example:

> I did see earlier subtitles as well as the original dubbed version. It was immediately clear that they were useless—little or no colloquial flavor or invention. I never returned to them. . . . Capturing the texture of the dialogue and the slang was imperative. . . . Historically, subtitles were purely functional, never meant to provide anything other than basic narrative

information. Classic French films are often praised for their literary qualities, so it is counter-productive to ignore the subtleties of a film's dialogue.[40]

Borger's concept of subtitling was more elaborate than Crowther's, informed by a historically grounded sense that led him to adopt a different practice. But although he saw his translation as exceeding "basic narrative information," his comments stop at maintaining an equivalence to the "literary qualities" of the dialogue, especially the use of slang. When the restored print was theatrically released in 2000, Borger's work was not only noticeable but appreciated for its inventiveness. J. Hoberman, the critic for the *Village Voice*, observed that "the retranslated subtitles are flavorsome. In my favorite, a friendly thug welcomes a B-girl to his table with an expansive, 'Hello, kid, sit your moneymaker down.'"[41] Hoberman evaluated the subtitles both as a suggestive use of language ("flavorsome") and as a convincing interpretation of the character depicted in the audiovisual image (the "expansive" remark fitting "a friendly thug").

Nonetheless, the foregoing comments, whether made by Borger or by the film critics, are limited by their concentration on the relationship between the translation and the dialogue on the soundtrack. If, however, we consider the relationship between the translation and the receiving culture, a broader interpretive context opens up, and Borger's work might continue to signify beyond the equivalence or stylistic approximation that he intended. The style that he cultivates in his subtitles belongs to specific literary and film genres: it consists of the underworld argot that derives from the hard-boiled prose used in United States crime fiction as well as in Hollywood film noir. For the informed viewer, in fact, Borger's subtitles may well recall John Huston's 1950 film, *The Asphalt Jungle*, which also focuses on a jewelry shop robbery with a tragic ending.[42] At points, the stylistic resemblance is striking: in Huston's film, when the ex-convict known as Dix tells his friend Gus that he "can't afford to knock off" robberies because of a gambling debt, Gus replies, "Oh, stop worrying. I'll stake you," using the same term that Borger's translation assigned to Tony in *Rififi*.

Such connections can set going the critical dialectic between the subtitles and the film that is always a latent possibility in reading a translation. The nature of the dialectic depends on the knowledge of cultural traditions and debates that the viewer brings to a viewing experience. In the case of *Rififi*, the contrast between the French spoken on the soundtrack and the nonstandard English of Borger's subtitles can heighten their sheer Americanness while invoking the intertextual and intersemiotic connections in which his translation is caught up.

Those connections can in turn indicate that the cultural conditions of *Rififi* are not only heterogeneous but transnational, both French and American. The film adapts Auguste Le Breton's crime novel, *Du rififi chez les hommes* (1953), which deploys French underworld argot, but it also reflects Dassin's work for Hollywood studios in the late 1940s, when he directed several films noir—*Brute Force* (1947), *The Naked City* (1948), *Thieves' Highway* (1949), *Night and the City* (1950)—before he was blacklisted in the McCarthy era and emigrated to France. Borger's subtitles call attention to the status of Dassin's *Rififi* as "world cinema" in Dudley Andrew's definition of that term: a key film, produced in a specific locale, which reveals "a conflicted cinematic vocabulary and grammar."[43] In *Rififi* two film tendencies, French poetic realism and Hollywood noir, form a compelling but uneasy synthesis. Thus Alastair Phillips recognizes "a porous sense of identity and lack of coherence regarding key aspects of its film style," perhaps most visible in the depiction of the spaces that Tony inhabits: although the film is set in Paris, "in moving through the doorway of his poetic realist apartment to the hubbub of the American style big city, [Tony] exemplifies the hybrid tensions of the film as a whole."[44]

Any subtitles can be seen as worlding a film by enabling it to cross national boundaries and circulate in other linguistic and cultural communities. Yet Borger's subtitles for *Rififi* go further not only by developing a noir style that contributes to characterization and narrative, but also by exposing the unique synthesis of local and foreign materials that constitute world cinema under the domination of Hollywood forms and practices. These interpretive possibilities would have been preempted if Borger had chosen to follow subtitling conventions by applying the manipulative strategies that reduce dialogue to basic narrative information and by adhering mostly to current standard English.

How Foreign Is It?

The inventive translations of Henri Béhar and Lenny Borger call to mind Abé Mark Nornes's pioneering distinction between "corrupt" and "abusive" subtitles. Nornes argues that the material conditions of subtitling, an "apparatus" of spatiotemporal constraints which "necessitates a violent translation of the source text," allow for two approaches: corrupt subtitlers "hide their repeated acts of violence through codified rules and a tradition of suppression," what I have been calling conventional subtitling practices, whereas "the abusive subtitler uses textual and graphic abuse—that is, experimentation with language and its grammatical, morphological, and visual qualities—to bring the fact of translation from its position of obscurity," turning precisely those subtitling conventions into the object of the abuse.[45] The term "corrupt" implies that Nornes's distinction constitutes an ethics of translation, and he frames the ethical significance of each approach in relation to the linguistic and cultural differences of the source material: corrupt subtitling is bad because it "domesticates all otherness while it pretends to bring the audience to an experience of the foreign," whereas abusive subtitling is good because it "strives to translate from and within the place of the other," an aim that has been understood by a scholar of audiovisual translation like Pérez-González as "providing unmediated access to the source culture."[46]

Since the subtitling strategies that Nornes describes as abusive deploy nonstandard linguistic items like slang, archaism, and obscenity, the work of Béhar and Borger would seem to be exemplary of that approach. Yet they rather lead us to rethink Nornes's account. Their subtitles show, first of all, that there is really no such place in a translation as "the place of the other" which remains unaffected by the translation process. When translated, "the other," the source material, the source culture are accessible only in mediated forms, never directly but through an interpretive act that derives from and answers to the receiving culture. It cannot be the case, then, that "abusive subtitles always direct spectators back to the original text."[47] For the Anglophone viewer of *Rififi* who cannot understand spoken French, Borger's subtitles are likely to point, at least initially, to United States crime fiction and Hollywood noir. If a viewer can manage a comparison between the subtitles and the soundtrack while viewing the film, Borger's choices will actually be found to increase the quantity of underworld argot beyond what occurs in the French dialogue. Nornes himself admits that mediation is inescapable in translation: on more than one occasion he states not only that the reductive or transformative "violence" of subtitling is "necessitated by the apparatus," but also that the foreignness of a foreign film can be registered only through subtitles that "bend the rules, both linguistic and cinematic."[48] We need to keep in mind that whatever practices the abusive subtitler uses to bend those rules, they originate in the receiving culture, like the rules themselves, not in the source culture.

Here a second problem with Nornes's account surfaces: his assumption of a viewing audience that is receptive to the abuse. Not only must the subtitler depart from conventional practices, but the viewer must perform an interpretive act to formulate the significance of the departure, its precise role in signaling the linguistic and cultural differences of the source material in the terms of the translating language and culture. Nornes takes for granted the viewer's ability to perceive and process the abuse, defined as "textual and cinematic effects that exceed the creation of a narrative-focused equivalence."[49] To the avid film viewer, Borger's slangy translation may certainly become noticeable in relation to subtitling conventions. But, whatever its effects may be, it still provides basic narrative information and can therefore be subsumed into the diegesis, so that for many viewers the subtitles will transparently support the realist illusion. Nornes seems to recognize this likelihood when he remarks that abusive subtitling "is directed at convention, even at spectators and their expectations."[50] Viewers must, in effect, be disabused of their expectations for an illusionistic response if they are to appreciate the interpretive potential of subtitles. Yet the countervailing power of subtitling conventions cannot be underestimated, insofar as they are housed in film distribution companies and translator training programs and validated by film critics, translation instructors, and subtitlers themselves. Such institutional forces will be difficult to dislodge or challenge if viewers are not somehow schooled in alternative practices of reception. This fact is borne out by the destiny of Béhar's subtitles for *Thérèse*: virtual oblivion.

Can subtitles be so abusive as to break free of the diegesis, momentarily shattering the illusion of reality and forcing the viewer to develop an interpretation of the audiovisual image that encompasses but exceeds the narrative? Nornes argues that "fansubbing" offers a paradigmatic case: since the 1990s, as developments in digital technology have allowed amateurs to subtitle films and television programs, their subtitles have resorted to such abusive strategies as "headnotes" that gloss the audiovisual image and typographical experiments with font, size, and color.[51] "The fansubbing subculture," Pérez-González observes, "often relies on combinations of diegetic subtitles conveying the meaning of the original spoken dialogue and unconventional titles incorporating a non-diegetic dimension into the subtitled text," blurring "the distinction between consuming a text and re-authoring it."[52]

This blurring may explain, at least partly, why the film industry has not enthusiastically welcomed fansubbing practices: they entail copyright infringement by turning consumers into producers who circulate their work on the internet through blogs and social media. Yet setting aside such legal considerations, we might notice more translatorly risks. In mixing elements that possess an unequal ontological status in relation to the image, diegetic vs. nondiegetic, funsubbing juxtaposes two different kinds of writing, interlingual translation vs. autonomous commentary. This juxtaposition undermines or even removes the need to develop innovative *translation* practices: fansubbers typically add titles that define source-language words, explain the significance of source-culture allusions and objects, and annotate the narrative, setting, and characterization, whereby they effectively compensate for the limitations of titles that concentrate on rendering the speech on the soundtrack. The question then remains: can *translators* be so resourceful as to produce subtitles that solicit the viewer's interpretation?

Consider the English subtitles of Park Chan-wook's horror film, *Bakjwi* (*Bat*, 2009), which has been released in Anglophone cultures as *Thirst*.[53] Most of the subtitles were written by Esther Kwon, a Toronto-based translator who since 2002 has subtitled over 150 Korean feature films in addition to translating shorts, television programs, screenplays, trailers, and press kits.[54] Additional subtitles were written by Wonjo Jeong, who has worked as a producer on Park Chan-wook's films. At several points, the subtitles of *Thirst* are so unexpected as to be distancing, if not simply disorienting, resisting any easy or immediate subsumption into the diegesis and making extraordinary hermeneutic demands on the viewer.

The main character is Sang-hyun, a Catholic priest who ministers to patients in a hospital. In the opening scene, he stands at the bedside of the terminally ill Hyo-sun, who relates how one day he was carrying a cake he longed to eat but finally decided to give it to two "starving" sisters. He wonders whether his good deed will be recognized after his death:

HYO-SUN: Think God will remember that?

Though it's been 30 years?

SANG-HYUN: Absoposilutely.

Remembering is His specialty.

Wonjo Jeong chose the word "absoposilutely" to translate the Korean on the soundtrack, "dang-geun-iji," a slang phrase that might be closely rendered as "it's a carrot" ("dang-guen" means "carrot"), but that has come to communicate an emphatic affirmation, such as "of course," "sure," "certainly," or "absolutely." Over the past two decades, the phrase was used first in youth culture and later more widely. Jeong's choice of "absoposilutely" establishes a semantic correspondence, but it simultaneously applies a thematic interpretant that aims to figure in not only the social origins of the Korean phrase but also the main character's psychology and the circumstances of his first appearance. In an interview Jeong explained his reasoning:

I noted how this was the first line of dialogue for the protagonist, Sang-hyun. It would form our first impression of the character. What is the auteur conveying? That the priest is cheerful, he is compassionate, he wants to be friendly. He may be overly cheerful even, employing the funny slang he picked up from kids. The priest is trying cheer up someone in a terrible condition, even resorting to using some lame humour.[55]

Jeong's translation practice assumes a hermeneutic model, he has interpreted the character in some detail, but like many professional subtitlers he treats his verbal choice instrumentally as reproducing a semantic invariant that is contained in the screenplay and expressed in the dialogue on the soundtrack. Thus in the interview he added that "it was all about preserving the author's intention and staying most faithful to it, to convey all the nuances and subtleties." Jeong's invocation of auteur theory complements his essentialist thinking about translation: the film is taken to be the container of an invariant form or meaning intended by the director, who in this case also cowrote the screenplay.[56]

Jeong's striking choice, however, continues to signify beyond any meaning his instrumentalism might assign to it, whether through his own interpretation or through his claim to be "preserving" the director's intention. Formed by the linguistic operation known as "infixation," in which a word in whole or in part is embedded in the body of another word,[57] "absoposilutely" inserts the first two syllables of "positive" after the first two syllables of "absolutely." It has gained limited currency in American English since the start of the present century, appearing in such diverse media as a Hollywood animated film (*The Tigger Movie* [2000]), a Japanese video game (*Phoenix Wright: Ace Attorney* [2001]), a 2003 entry on UrbanDictionary.com, and a 2007 submission to the website for the Merriam-Webster dictionary, among various internet-based advertisements and forums. The contexts where the word has been used suggest that in addition to its core meaning (emphatic affirmation) it can carry connotations of eccentricity, childishness, playfulness, foolishness, even ridiculousness, complicating any interpretation of Sang-hyun's characterization in the opening scene. A more suspicious viewer might consider the subtitle, not as a cheerful expression of the priest's compassion, but rather as an ironic indication of his naïve idealism. When he speaks the Korean phrase, he smiles broadly as if to allay Hyo-sun's spiritual doubt in the face of his approaching death. But the sheer goofiness of the subtitle can imply that Sang-hyun has missed the real motivation behind Hyo-sun's question: the overweight patient suffers from a guilty conscience, especially after offering a gluttonous description of the cake he surrendered.

"Absoposilutely" emerges as a point of indeterminacy that can be reduced to a univocal meaning and folded into the diegesis, but that can also resonate with irony and unsettle the realist illusion. Although it maintains a semantic correspondence with the Korean slang, it is a neologism that deviates from subtitling conventions which favor current standard English. Whether because of this deviation or the unfamiliarity of the word or both factors, "absoposilutely" takes Anglophone viewers by surprise. In 2011 Stan Carey, the author of a blog devoted to topics in linguistics, observed that "I didn't expect to see *absoposilutely* in the subtitles of a Korean horror film," a reaction that was shared by his commentators.[58] That surprise definitely moves some viewers to develop an interpretation of the subtitle. Carey's blog drew a comment from a "Korean speaker" who understood the "kids' slang" on the soundtrack and explained that "the translator probably wished to keep the effect of a rather unexpected use of a childish play on pronunciation." A nonstandard item in a subtitle is thus capable of making the translator visible to viewers who may then feel compelled, depending on their linguistic proficiency and hermeneutic competence, to interpret the translation in relation to the soundtrack, shifting between diegetic and nondiegetic levels of the film.

By far the most jolting subtitles in *Thirst* involve colloquialism and obscenity. I will cite two instances that show the translator Esther Kwon making verbal choices that far exceed the establishment of a semantic correspondence. In the first, drawn from an early scene set in a church, Sang-hyun is hearing the confession of a nurse who contemplates suicide after a romantic breakup. He provides pastoral counseling, assigns her prayers for penance, and advises such earthly remedies as sunbathing, a cold shower, and antidepressants. The formal tone of his speech abruptly changes, however, when he adds, "And . . . forget the bastard who dumped you" ("Geurigo ddeonan-nom-eun ijeobeoryeo ije jom"; Kwon added the ellipsis). The choice of "dumped" colloquializes the Korean "ddeonan," which might be translated with such standard items as "left" or "abandoned," while the obscenity "bastard" is used for the Korean "nom," a derogatory term that might be translated into a variety of English words, including colloquialisms like "jerk," "bum," "creep," or "cad," as well as "bastard." Kwon clearly chose the alternative that is not only the most intense, but also the most likely to produce a shock effect on the viewer insofar as it is uttered by a priest performing the sacrament of penance in a confessional.

The second instance occurs later, after Sang-hyun becomes reacquainted with his childhood friend, Kang-woo, who is now married to Tae-ju. The scene occurs in the kitchen of their home as Tae-ju prepares gimbap, rice rolled in laver seaweed, and her mother-in-law Mrs. Ra speaks with the priest. Tae-ju interrupts their conversation to address Mrs. Ra, and the subtitles give the following translation over two frames, two lines to each frame:

Why'd you buy the laver
at that place again, Mom?
I told you it's no good
and the owner's a cocksucker.

The English obscenity intensifies the Korean word on the
soundtrack, "gaesaekki," which might be translated as "son of
a bitch," although neither Mrs. Ra nor Sang-hyun acknowledges
in any way the milder Korean obscenity. Perhaps for this very
reason, "cocksucker" seems all the more astonishing: not only
is it inappropriate in the domestic setting, particularly in the
presence of a priest, but for a moment its unexpected extremity
breaks out of the diegesis, seemingly lacking any relation to
the scene.

In an interview Kwon was unable to provide detailed expla-
nations for her choices, noting that she worked on the project
"so long ago."[59] Nonetheless, she did see her subtitles as offering
interpretations of the characters. "I used more colloquial terms
here [in the confession scene] to show Sang-hyun as 'the not-
your-average-priest,'" she stated, and "we [she and the director]
decided to go with this word ["cocksucker"] to make a strong
first impression of Tae-ju." Yet when Kwon described her general aim as a translator, she suppressed any differences that her
interpretations might have introduced between the soundtrack
and her subtitles by invoking a concept of equivalent effect and
therefore by assuming an instrumental model of translation:
"Rather than being divided as viewers and readers (of the subtitles)," she asserted, "my goal is for the audience (as one) to
have the same experience in watching the films."

This goal seems unachievable. There can be no doubt
that viewers who are capable of comprehending the Korean
soundtrack do not experience the same film as those who must
read Kwon's subtitles. In the kitchen scene, for instance, the

key differences involve not only the harsh obscenity in the English, but also the deletion of various polite honorifics from the Korean. An English version that is closer to the soundtrack, although it risks sarcasm that is not present in Tae-ju's speech, might be formulated as follows: "I respectfully mentioned, Ma'am, that the seaweed tears too easily, and the storeowner is a real son of a bitch." Kwon drastically condensed the Korean, removing a pronoun ("je"), a noun ("malsseum"), a verb stem ("deuli"), and a suffix ("-yo"), all of which a Korean viewer would recognize as Tae-ju's effort to show politeness and respect toward her mother-in-law. These items heighten Tae-ju's incongruous use of an obscenity like "gaesaekki" (son of a bitch), the rudeness of which would seem to displace her resentment of Mrs. Ra onto the storeowner she patronizes. Tae-ju's speech can be seen as expressing her inferior status in the family as well as her dissatisfaction: on the one hand, she is acutely aware that her uneducated father abandoned her at three years old with Mrs. Ra, who raised her to become Kang-woo's wife; on the other hand, she chafes at the repression and mistreatment she has suffered from her mother-in-law and husband. The family hierarchy is reflected spatially in the mise-en-scène: Tae-ju sits on the floor in the foreground preparing a meal, whereas Mrs. Ra sits on a chair at the table in the background explaining her daughter-in-law's history to Sang-hyun.

The viewer who must depend on the subtitles is likely to interpret the scenes differently so as to maintain or restore the coherence of the diegesis. The colloquialism and obscenity can be read as revealing the characters' personalities, their tendency to vulgarity, abuse, and immorality, and therefore as anticipating later narrative developments. All of those traits are spectacularly displayed after Sang-hyun becomes a vampire through a contaminated blood transfusion, engages in a lustful affair with Tae-ju, conspires with her to murder her husband, and ultimately infects her with his vampirism. Tae-ju's intention to offend her mother-in-law would be clear enough in her use of "cocksucker," but the word magnifies her resentment to such an extent that the realist illusion is destabilized, particularly since she has just used a homely term like "mom."

In that instant, a viewer immersed in traditions of Hollywood horror might recall an equally startling use of the same obscenity in William Friedkin's film of demonic possession, *The Exorcist* (1973), where it is assigned to twelve-year-old Regan MacNeil.[60] The demon, speaking through Regan, shouts at the priest who conducts the exorcism: "Stick your cock up her ass, you motherfucking worthless cocksucker!" Once perceived, the intertextual connection between the two films can solicit further interpretation: it suggests that Tae-ju is inherently evil while exposing the conventionality of Friedkin's film in distinguishing between the demon, on the one hand, and the possessed girl and her ministering priests, on the other. In Park's film, any such distinctions are erased: it is a mistreated young woman and a self-sacrificing priest who become the demonic beings.

The intertext established by the subtitle can lead the viewer to recognize the cultural difference of *Thirst*, its participation in what critics have called Korean "extreme" film and hence its foreignness in relation to the Hollywood filmmaking practices that also inform it. "Although contemporary South Korean films share a set of common stylistic devices and high productive values with Hollywood blockbusters," Robert Cagle has remarked, "South Korean films rarely, if ever, conform to the same narrative codes," so that "the refusal of these works to identify characters with moral positions drawn along distinct and unwavering lines is clearly critical of the overwhelmingly dominant American model."[61] The English subtitles for *Thirst* point to its transnational conditions: as the product of a minor culture, it occupies a subordinate position in the hierarchy of cultural resources and prestige that constitutes world cinema, but it also submits that hierarchy to interrogation by transforming a Hollywood genre like horror. That transformation turned out to be effective in earning Park's film the consecration that only institutions in major cultures can give through practices like translation and award-giving: it won the Jury Prize at the 2009 Cannes Film Festival.

The trouble with subtitles, I conclude, is a matter of interpretation—in all the senses that I have tried to construe "interpretation" in this chapter. Subtitles themselves inscribe interpretations of the speech on the soundtrack, whether the translator works within or challenges conventional subtitling practices. Yet these interpretations tend to remain invisible at every stage in the production and reception of a subtitled film or television program because distributors and translators, translation scholars and instructors, critics and viewers assume an instrumental model of translation. This model underlies the range of manipulative practices that are currently used in subtitling as well as the restriction to the current standard dialect of the translating language so as to produce an illusion of linguistic transparency that supports the realist illusion of the diegesis. Instrumentalism has prevented translators and viewers alike from performing their own interpretive acts by emphasizing basic narrative information and thereby constraining the theoretical sophistication and imaginative resourcefulness that would be much more appreciative of the potential effects of subtitles.

The recent introduction of so-called multimodal transcription in training subtitlers would seem to indicate an advance, since it aims to base the translation on the entire audiovisual image, not merely the speech on the soundtrack. It thus understands that "audiovisual communication," as Pérez-González observes, "consists in the production and interpretation of an ensemble of semiotic modalities that are made available via the synchronized use of multiple media."[62] Yet the application of this methodology has been impaired by continued adherence to subtitling conventions and by simplistic notions of interpretation, such as when the analysis begins with a statement of the "overriding message" of the film.[63] This move effectively takes one interpretation as a semantic invariant and preempts other interpretive possibilities that might also be substantiated by the same audiovisual image.

Isn't it time that we acknowledged instrumentalism to be a hoax, born out of the fear that translation contaminates and falsifies when it ought to reproduce or transfer a source invariant? Translation can definitely give us a semantic correspondence, it can even approximate the style of the source material, but it does not do either without the variation that an interpretation always introduces. The source material, moreover, like any cultural form or practice, can support multiple and conflicting interpretations, and so different translations are possible, each one guided by semantic correspondence and stylistic approximation even when they also cultivate different registers, dialects, and discourses. A translation is a cultural artifact with its own constitutive materials and its own ways of processing them, with its own cultural and social effects and its own historical significance. That is something we should study and practice and, yes, learn how to enjoy.

STOP/START

After reading the foregoing polemic, you will no doubt have questions that I have not anticipated or answered, or you will simply want various points to be developed at greater, more nuanced length, perhaps in arguments that you might find more cogent. At this juncture, however, what concerns me most is not further exposition or argument but the sort of thinking about translation in which you have made your deepest investment—and whether the desiring-machine I have devised might have affected it. I am more concerned, in other words, with triggering change in your intellectual desire.

"A machine may be defined," write Deleuze and Guattari, "as a *system of interruptions* or breaks (*coupures*)," since "every machine, in the first place, is related to a continual material flow (*hylè*) that it cuts into" (their emphasis).[1] If my critique carries the potential of desiring-production that deterritorializes instrumentalism in translation theory and commentary, then it must provide instructions for interruption, not only for carrying out the critique but also for pursuing new ways of thinking about translation based on the hermeneutic model. Which concepts and practices must be avoided and which deployed to ensure that translation is conceived and performed as an interpretive act? What must be done to stop the flow of desire

to instrumentalism and divert it toward a hermeneutic understanding of translation?

The mode of address I will use to answer these questions
is imperative and frankly ideological, quite like propaganda,
issuing orders and inviting you "to adopt a position of struggle rather than stability."[2] This position is at once discursive
and institutional. It calls on you to resist the dominance of
instrumentalism in discourses housed in cultural institutions.

> STOP assuming that a source text possesses an invariant form,
> meaning, or effect; START assuming that a source text can
> support multiple and conflicting interpretations and therefore
> an equally heterogeneous succession of translations.

The instrumentalist assumption of invariance presupposes
direct, unmediated access to source-text features and effects
which, insofar as they can and should be reproduced or transferred, become the criteria by which translations are produced
and then assessed for "accuracy," "correctness," "fidelity." This
assumption masks the complex interpretive act by which both
translator and evaluator actually fix the form, meaning, and
effect of the source text and select a unit of translation to ground
an equivalence or a comparison with the translated text. Any
text, however, is a differential plurality that is always already
mediated even before a translation aims to create a semantic
correspondence and a stylistic approximation to that text.[3]

A translation may set up diverse relations of equivalence while
inscribing the source text with a variable interpretation that is
controlled by the institutions in which it is produced and circulated. A translation should be evaluated, then, according to the
degree of necessity that the translator establishes for an interpretation in relation not only to source-text features and effects but
also to the hierarchy of values, beliefs, and representations validated by those institutions. Our evaluation should ask whether

a translation contributes to the stable functioning of the arts and sciences in their current configuration or sets going a productive, even if destabilized, process of innovation and change.

> STOP thinking of source texts in terms of translatability and untranslatability and of translation as involving loss or gain; START thinking of translation as an interpretive act that can be performed on any source text.

A translation can be seen as incurring a loss of source-text features and effects only if they are assumed to be invariants that the translation must reproduce or transfer. Yet no translation can perform this task: linguistic and cultural differences ensure that it always submits the source text to a transformation that is simultaneously decontextualizing and recontextualizing, that alters and replaces the signifying process of the source text with another signifying process in the translating language. Hence the meanings, values, and functions that the source text supports in its originary culture ultimately give way to those that the translation supports in the receiving culture.

This shift in signification, which is indivisibly both linguistic and cultural, does not result in a gain to the source text. The notion of gain, like that of loss, is an instrumentalist metaphor that assumes invariant features and effects against which a gain can be measured. Translation rather constructs a different context of interpretation through the application of various interpretants, both formal and thematic, creating new possibilities of reception for the source text in a different language and culture. Just as any text can be interpreted, so can any text be translated—unless the understanding of translation is restricted by an assumption of invariance.

> STOP reading translations as if they were or could be identical to their source texts; START reading translations as

texts in their own right, relatively autonomous from the texts they translate.

More often than not translations are read because of their source texts, not because of the interpretations they inscribe in those texts. Today this practice is universal: reading is bound by inescapable limitations on foreign-language proficiency so that every reader must use translations from many languages, not just readers in aggressively monolingual cultures like the United States, but also readers in multilingual cultures like Africa and India. As a result, translations constantly risk a reduction to their source texts, if not simply an erasure of any distinction between them, especially given the worldwide dominance of instrumentalist thinking about translation.

Current translation practices that require translators to maintain a semantic correspondence and stylistic approximation enable a translation to provide some sense of source-text form and meaning. But this sense can only be limited: translation is radically transformative. To develop a critical consciousness of this fact and forestall the reduction of a translation to its source text, different assumptions must be applied in reading translations. Readers must assume that the translator's verbal choices constitute interpretive moves, rewriting the source text with formal and semantic features that are specific to the receiving culture and its institutions.[4] Perhaps most importantly, translators must be able to give a sophisticated account of their interpretive acts to the various readerships who rely on their work, both elite and popular, so as to support the development of a translation literacy.

I am acutely aware of having outlined a struggle that may seem so difficult as to be regarded as impossible, if it is not merely dismissed as pointless or irrelevant. Intellectual habits have established a seemingly commonsensical view of translation that at this point is assumed to be indisputable. Nothing can appear more natural than to read a translation as giving back the source text so that to posit a crucial difference between them may come off as implausible. Nothing can appear more natural than to compare one word or phrase in the translation to its counterpart in the source text so as to judge the efficacy of the translation. Any insinuation that a third term or an entire set of factors must be present for the comparison to take place may come off as a needless complication. And of course nothing seems more natural than to continue these habits in producing, circulating, and using translations as well as in studying and teaching translation practices.

Yet nothing can be more naïve in the effort to understand what a translation is and does.

The habits must be exposed for the utter anti-intellectualism they sustain, along with the damage they have long done to translation as well as to its status in cultural institutions.

And so I ask: Where is your desire? Is it invested in the instrumentalism that has dominated thinking about translation from time immemorial? Or are you ready to stop repressing the difficult questions that translation raises, to examine the linguistic and cultural differences that it is summoned to negotiate but always proliferates, and to explore the interpretive power that it commands to change forms and practices, discourses and institutions?

Where is your desire?

NOTES

START/STOP

1. See Charles S. Peirce, *The Writings of Charles S. Peirce: A Chronological Edition, 1867–1871*, ed. Edward C. Moore (Bloomington: Indiana University Press, 1984), 2:53–54; Umberto Eco, *A Theory of Semiotics* (Bloomington: Indiana University Press, 1976), 15, 69–71; and Eco, "Peirce's Notion of Interpretant," MLN 91, no. 6 (1976): 1457–72.

2. See Jacques Derrida, "Violence and Metaphysics: An Essay on the Thought of Emmanuel Levinas," in *Writing and Difference*, trans. Alan Bass (Chicago: University of Chicago Press, 1978), 115, and Rodolphe Gasché, *The Tain of the Mirror: Derrida and the Philosophy of Reflection* (Cambridge MA: Harvard University Press, 1986), 161.

3. See Jacques Derrida, "Signature Event Context," in *Margins of Philosophy*, trans. Alan Bass (Chicago: University of Chicago Press, 1982), 320.

4. Martin Heidegger, "The Anaximander Fragment," in *Early Greek Thinking*, trans. David Farrell Krell and Frank A. Capuzzi (New York: Harper & Row, 1975), 14.

5. Heidegger, "The Anaximander Fragment," 22.

6. Heidegger, "The Anaximander Fragment," 22.

7. Heidegger, "The Anaximander Fragment," 30.

8. Martin Heidegger, "Der Spruch des Anaximander," in *Holzwege* (Frankfurt: Klostermann, 1950), 337.

9. Henry George Liddell and Robert Scott, *A Greek-English Lexicon*, rev. ed. Sir Henry Stuart Jones with Roderick McKenzie (Oxford: Clarendon Press, 1940), s.vv. "γένεσις" and "Φθορά."

10. See Mark A. Wrathall, *Heidegger and Unconcealment: Truth, Language, and History* (Cambridge: Cambridge University Press, 2011).

11. Heidegger, "The Anaximander Fragment," 57; "Der Spruch des Anaximander," 367.

12. I have considered these origins in two articles: "Genealogies of Translation Theory: Jerome," *boundary 2* 37, no. 3 (2010): 5–28, and "Genealogies of Translation Theory: Schleiermacher and the Hermeneutic Model," in *Un/Translatables: New Maps for Germanic Literatures*, ed. Bethany Wiggin and Catriona MacLeod (Evanston IL: Northwestern University Press, 2016), 45–62.

13. See Michel Foucault, *The Archaeology of Knowledge and the Discourse on Language*, trans. A. M. Sheridan Smith (New York: Random House, 1972), part 4.

14. Michel Foucault, *The Order of Things: An Archaeology of the Human Sciences* (New York: Random House, 1970), xxii, 168. No translator is credited, although Alan Sheridan lists this text as one of his translations on his website: http://alansheridanauthor.com/translation-philosphy.html.

15. Foucault, *The Order of Things*, xi.

16. Foucault, *The Order of Things*, xi; *The Archaeology of Knowledge*, 38.

17. Eugene Nida, *Towards a Science of Translating, with Special Reference to Principles and Procedures Involved in Bible Translating* (Leiden: Brill, 1964), 159.

18. Keith Harvey, "A Descriptive Framework for Compensation," *The Translator* 1, no. 1 (1995): 66.

19. Harvey, "A Descriptive Framework for Compensation," 68.

20. Friedrich Schleiermacher, "On the Different Methods of Translating" (1813), trans. Susan Bernofsky, in *The Translation Studies Reader*, 3rd ed., ed. Lawrence Venuti (Abingdon UK: Routledge, 2012), 49. The German is cited from Friedrich Schleiermacher, "Über die verschiedenen Methoden des Übersetzens," in *Schriften und Entwürfe: Akademievorträge*, ed. Martin Rössler with Lars Emersleben (Berlin: Walter de Gruyter, 2002), 74.

21. Schleiermacher, "On the Different Methods of Translating," 53; "Über die verschiedenen Methoden des Übersetzens," 81.

22. Foucault, *The Archaeology of Knowledge*, 192.

23. John Dryden, "Preface to Ovid's *Epistles*" (1680), in *The Works of John Dryden*, ed. E. N. Hooker and H. T. Swedenberg, Jr. (Berkeley: University of California Press, 1956), 1:114, 116.

24. Dryden, "Preface to Ovid's *Epistles*," 117.

25. Foucault, *The Archaeology of Knowledge*, 155, 153. The italics are Foucault's.

26. Foucault, *The Archaeology of Knowledge*, 154. The italics are Foucault's.

27. Basil Hatim and Ian Mason, *The Translator as Communicator* (London: Routledge, 1997), 12.

28. Foucault, *The Archaeology of Knowledge*, 153. The italics are Foucault's.

29. Foucault, *The Archaeology of Knowledge*, 153.

30. Foucault, *The Archaeology of Knowledge*, 175.

31. Hatim and Mason, *The Translator as Communicator*, 20.

32. Hatim and Mason, *The Translator as Communicator*, 1.

33. André Lefevere, "Mother Courage's Cucumbers: Text, System and Refraction in a Theory of Literature," *Modern Language Studies* 12, no. 4 (1982): 4–7.

34. Lefevere, "Mother Courage's Cucumbers," 4.

35. Lefevere, "Mother Courage's Cucumbers," 4.

36. Lefevere, "Mother Courage's Cucumbers," 10.

37. Lefevere, "Mother Courage's Cucumbers," 10–13.

38. Lefevere, "Mother Courage's Cucumbers," 14.

39. See, for example, Allan Antliff, "Poetic Tension, Artistic Cruelty: Paul Goodman, Antonin Artaud, and the Living Theatre," *Anarchist Developments in Cultural Studies* 1–2 (2015): 3–30, https://journals.uvic .ca/index.php/adcs/article/view/17179.

40. Foucault, *The Order of Things*, xi. The italics are Foucault's.

41. I discuss this anti-intellectualism in *Translation Changes Everything: Theory and Practice* (Abingdon UK: Routledge, 2013), 61–69, 231–43.

42. See, for example, the contrast between Dawn Tsang, "Translator as Co-Producer: Metempsychosis and Metamorphosis in Ezra Pound's *Cathay*," *Asia Pacific Translation and Intercultural Studies* 1, no. 2 (2014): 142–70, and Dominic Cheetham, "Literary Translation and Conceptual Metaphors: From Movement to Performance," *Translation Studies* 9, no. 3 (2016): 241–55.

43. Wyatt Mason, "Homer's Daughter," *New York Times Magazine*, November 5, 2017, 50.

44. Mason, "Homer's Daughter," 51.

45. I discuss retranslations along these lines in *Translation Changes Everything*, 96–108.

46. Frederick Rener gathers citations in *Interpretatio: Language and Translation from Cicero to Tytler* (Amsterdam: Benjamins, 1989), 24–26. See also A. E. B. Coldiron, "Commonplaces and Metaphors," in *The Oxford History of Literary Translation in English, Volume 2, 1550–1660*, ed. Gordon Braden, Robert Cummings, and Stuart Gillespie (Oxford: Oxford University Press, 2011), 112.

47. George Chapman, "The Preface to the Reader," in *Chapman's Homer: The Iliad, Odyssey and the Lesser Homerica*, ed. Allardyce Nicholl (Princeton NJ: Princeton University Press, 1956), 1:17.

48. See Siobhán McElduff, *Roman Theories of Translation: Surpassing the Source* (Abingdon UK: Routledge, 2013), chap. 4; Rita Copeland, *Rhetoric, Hermeneutics, and Translation in the Middle Ages: Academic Traditions and Vernacular Texts* (Cambridge: Cambridge University Press, 1991), chap. 1; A. C. Howell, "*Res et Verba*: Words and Things," *ELH* 13, no. 2 (1946): 131–42; Rener, *Interpretatio*, 19–24.

49. Cicero, *De invention; De optimo genere oratorum; Topica*, ed. and trans. H. M. Hubbell (Cambridge MA: Harvard University Press, 1949), 5:14. The early modern meanings of Chapman's Latinisms are listed in the *Oxford English Dictionary*, s.v. "convert, v.," III.13 and "interpreter, n.," 2.a.

50. For "apt" in the early modern sense of "fitted (materially)," see the *Oxford English Dictionary*, s.v. "apt, adj.," 1.

51. For the early modern sense of "convert" as "to change in character or function," see the *Oxford English Dictionary*, s.v. "convert, v.," II.c.

52. Foucault, *The Order of Things*, 29, 32.

53. Alexander Fraser Tytler, *Essay on the Principles of Translation*, ed. Jeffrey Hunstman (Amsterdam: Benjamins, 1978), 110.

54. Foucault, *The Order of Things*, 64.

55. Foucault, *The Order of Things*, 281.

56. Walter Benjamin, "The Translator's Task," trans. Steven Rendall, in Venuti, *The Translation Studies Reader*, 78.

57. Benjamin, "The Translator's Task," 78.

58. Benjamin, "The Translator's Task," 77–78.

59. Benjamin, "The Translator's Task," 75, 77, 79, 80; Benjamin, "Die Aufgabe des Übersetzers," in *Gesammelte Schriften IV*, ed. Tillman Rexroth (Frankfurt: Suhrkamp, 1972), 1:9, 12.

60. Benjamin, "The Translator's Task," 79.

61. Benjamin, "The Translator's Task," 79.

62. Benjamin, "The Translator's Task," 79. The quotation incorporates emendations that translator Steven Rendall made to the published version of this passage in email correspondence (December 20, 2017).

63. Benjamin, "The Translator's Task," 81.

64. Benjamin, "The Translator's Task," 79, 80, 83; Benjamin, "Die Aufgabe des Übersetzers," 1:14, 21.

65. Benjamin, "The Translator's Task," 76, 81, 83.

66. Beatrice Hanssen, "Language and Mimesis in Walter Benjamin's Work," in *The Cambridge Companion to Walter Benjamin*, ed. David S. Ferris (Cambridge: Cambridge University Press, 2004), 56.

67. Michel Foucault, "What Is Enlightenment?," trans. Catherine Porter, in *The Foucault Reader*, ed. Paul Rabinow (New York: Pantheon, 1984), 46.

68. The Metropolitan Museum of Art, "Mark Polizzotti Named Publisher & Editor in Chief," news release, November 10, 2010, https:// www.metmuseum.org/press/news/2010/mark-polizzotti-named -publisher—editor-in-chief-at-the-metropolitan-museum-of-art.

69. FACE Foundation, "French Voices Catalogue," http://face-foundation .org/french-voices/.

70. Mark Polizzotti, *Sympathy for the Traitor: A Translation Manifesto* (Cambridge MA: MIT Press, 2018), xiii, xv.

71. Polizzotti, *Sympathy for the Traitor*, 8.

72. Polizzotti, *Sympathy for the Traitor*, 16.

73. Polizzotti, *Sympathy for the Traitor*, 78.

74. Polizzotti, *Sympathy for the Traitor*, 63.

75. Polizzotti, *Sympathy for the Traitor*, 106.

76. Mark Cousins, *The Story of Film* (London: Pavilion, 2004), 145.

77. Polizzotti, *Sympathy for the Traitor*, 102–3.

78. I discuss the illusion of transparency in *The Translator's Invisibility: A History of Translation*, 2nd ed. (Abingdon UK: Routledge, 2008), 1–5.

79. Michael J. McGrath, "Tilting at Windmills: *Don Quijote* in English," *Cervantes: Bulletin of the Cervantes Society of America* 26, no. 1 (2006):

7–39; John Jay Allen, "*Traduttori Traditori: Don Quixote* in English," *Crítica Hispánica* 1, no. 1 (1979): 1–13.

80. McGrath, "Tilting at Windmills," 38.

81. McGrath, "Tilting at Windmills," 16, 15.

82. The actual title is *Diccionário De La Lengua Castellana: En Que Se Explica El Verdadero Sentido De Las Voces, Su Naturaleza Y Calidad, Con Las Phrases O Modos De Hablar, Los Proverbios O Refranes, Y Otras Cosas Convenientes Al Uso De La Lengua* (Madrid: Hierro, 1726–1739), 6 vols.

83. The meanings I have cited for "adarga" appear in the *Collins Spanish to English Dictionary*, https://www.collinsdictionary.com/dictionary/spanish-english/adarga; *Langensheidt's Pocket Spanish Dictionary* (Berlin: Langenscheidt, 1997); and *Oxford Language Dictionaries*, https://es.oxforddictionaries.com/translate/spanish-english/adarga.

84. Frank Kermode, "Institutional Control of Interpretation," in *The Art of Telling: Essays on Fiction* (Cambridge MA: Harvard University Press, 1985), 170.

85. McGrath, "Tilting at Windmills," 30.

86. McGrath, "Tilting at Windmills," 7.

87. Allen, "*Traduttori Tradutori*," 1.

88. Brian Mossop, "Invariance Orientation: Identifying an Object for Translation Studies," *Translation Studies* 10, no. 3 (2017): 329.

89. Mossop, "Invariance Orientation," 331.

90. Mossop, "Invariance Orientation," 331, 332.

91. Mossop, "Invariance Orientation," 331.

92. Mossop, "Invariance Orientation," 332.

93. Mossop, "Invariance Orientation," 331.

94. Mossop, "Invariance Orientation," 335.

95. Mossop, "Invariance Orientation," 335.

96. One way into these developments is Kathleen Davis's entry, "Deconstruction," in *Routledge Encyclopedia of Translation Studies*, 2nd ed., ed. Mona Baker and Gabriela Saldanha (Abingdon UK: Routledge, 2009), 74–77.

97. Mossop, "Invariance Orientation," 336.

98. Gilles Deleuze and Félix Guattari, *Anti-Oedipus: Capitalism and Schizophrenia*, trans. Robert Hurley, Mark Seem, and Helen R. Lane (Minneapolis: University of Minnesota Press, 1983), 1:1; *A Thousand*

Plateaus: Capitalism and Schizophrenia, trans. Brian Massumi (Minneapolis: University of Minnesota Press, 1987), 333–34, 504–5.

99. Deleuze and Guattari, *Anti-Oedipus*, 116, 183.

1. HIJACKING TRANSLATION

1. Pierre Bourdieu, *Homo Academicus*, trans. Peter Collier (Stanford CA: Stanford University Press, 1988), 94–95.

2. "The Greene Report, 1975: A Report on Standards," in *Comparative Literature in the Age of Multiculturalism*, ed. Charles Bernheimer (Baltimore: Johns Hopkins University Press, 1995), 30. The current figure for U.S.-based departments and programs was provided by Corinne Scheiner, who oversaw the 2014 *Report on the Undergraduate Comparative Literature Curriculum* for the Association of Departments and Programs of Comparative Literature (email correspondence, February 7, 2014).

3. Erich Auerbach, *Mimesis: The Representation of Reality in Western Literature*, trans. Willard R. Trask (Princeton NJ: Princeton University Press, 1953), 23; Auerbach, *Mimesis; dargestellte Wirklichkeit in der abendländischen Literatur* (Bern: A. Francke, 1946), 30.

4. "The Bernheimer Report, 1993: Comparative Literature at the Turn of the Century," in Bernheimer, *Comparative Literature in the Age of Multiculturalism*, 47.

5. "The Bernheimer Report, 1993," 44.

6. "The Bernheimer Report, 1993," 44.

7. Haun Saussy, ed., *Comparative Literature in an Age of Globalization* (Baltimore: Johns Hopkins University Press, 2006). This volume includes Steven Ungar's essay, "Writing in Tongues: Thoughts on the Work of Translation," 127–38.

8. Haun Saussy, "Exquisite Corpses from Fresh Nightmares: Of Memes, Hives and Selfish Genes," in Saussy, *Comparative Literature in an Age of Globalization*, 14.

9. Saussy, "Exquisite Corpses," 14.

10. Saussy, "Exquisite Corpses," 29.

11. Saussy, "Exquisite Corpses," 26.

12. Association of Departments and Programs of Comparative Literature, "2005 Report on the Undergraduate Comparative Literature Curriculum," in *Profession 2006* (New York: Modern Language Association, 2006), 181.

13. Ursula K. Heise, "Introduction: Comparative Literature and the New Humanities," in *Futures of Comparative Literature: ACLA State of the Discipline Report*, ed. Ursula K. Heise (Abingdon UK: Routledge, 2017), 2.

14. Haun Saussy, "Comparative Literature: The Next Ten Years," in Heise, *Futures of Comparative Literature*, 26.

15. Brigitte Rath, "Pseudotranslation," in Heise, *Futures of Comparative Literature*, 230. Rath cites Gideon Toury's discussion in *Descriptive Translation Studies—and Beyond* (Amsterdam: Benjamins, 1995), 40–52.

16. Shaden Tageldin, "Untranslatability," in Heise, *Futures of Comparative Literature*, 235.

17. Lucas Klein, "Reading and Speaking for Translation: De-institutionalizing the Institutions of Literary Study," in Heise, *Futures of Comparative Literature*, 216–17.

18. André Lefevere, "Mother Courage's Cucumbers: Text, System and Refraction in a Theory of Literature," *Modern Language Studies* 12, no. 4 (1982): 3–20; "Evaluating Translations as Scholarship: Guidelines for Peer Review," Modern Language Association, https://www.mla.org/About-Us/Governance/Executive-Council/Executive-Council-Actions/2011/Evaluating-Translations-as-Scholarship-Guidelines-for-Peer-Review.

19. Ursula K. Heise, "Comparative Literature and the Environmental Humanities," in Heise, *Futures of Comparative Literature*, 295.

20. Heise, "Comparative Literature and the Environmental Humanities," 295; Heise, "World Literature and the Environment," in *The Routledge Companion to World Literature*, ed. Theo D'haen, David Damrosch, and Djelal Kadir (Abingdon UK: Routledge, 2013), 405.

21. Daniela Kato and Bruce Allen, "Toward an Ecocritical Approach to Translation: A Conceptual Framework," in *State of the Discipline Report, American Comparative Literature Association*, posted March 3, 2014, https://stateofthediscipline.acla.org/entry/toward-ecocritical-approach-translation-conceptual-framework.

22. Pascale Casanova, *La République mondiale des Lettres* (Paris: Seuil, 1999); Casanova, *The World Republic of Letters*, trans. M. B. DeBevoise (Cambridge MA: Harvard University Press, 2004); Franco Moretti, "Conjectures on World Literature," *New Left Review* n.s. 1 (January–February 2000): 54–68.

23. Jahan Ramazani, *A Transnational Poetics* (Chicago: University of Chicago Press, 2009); Rebecca Walkowitz, *Born Translated: The Contemporary Novel in an Age of World Literature* (New York: Columbia University Press, 2015).

24. Walkowitz, *Born Translated*, 1, 98.

25. Walkowitz, *Born Translated*, 28.

26. David Damrosch, *What Is World Literature?* (Princeton NJ: Princeton University Press, 2003).

27. David Damrosch et al., eds., *The Longman Anthology of World Literature*, 6 vols. (New York: Longman, 2004).

28. "Goethe's Mignon," in *The Nineteenth Century*, vol. E of *The Longman Anthology of World Literature*, 2nd ed., ed. Marshall Brown and Bruce Robbins (New York: Longman, 2009), 198, 199.

29. Emily Apter, *Against World Literature: On the Politics of Untranslatability* (London: Verso, 2013), 3.

30. Apter, *Against World Literature*, 3, 8.

31. Apter, *Against World Literature*, 16.

32. Barbara Cassin, ed., *Vocabulaire européen des philosophies: Dictionnaire des intraduisables* (Paris: Seuil, 2004), xxi.

33. Barbara Cassin, ed., *Dictionary of Untranslatables: A Philosophical Lexicon*, trans. Steven Rendall et al., translation edited by Emily Apter, Jacques Lezra, and Michael Wood (Princeton NJ: Princeton University Press, 2014).

34. Cassin, *Vocabulaire européen des philosophies*, xviii.

35. Cassin, *Vocabulaire européen des philosophies*, xvii. The parenthesis is Cassin's.

36. Apter, *Against World Literature*, 32–33. The brackets are Apter's.

37. Apter, *Against World Literature*, 33.

38. Barbara Cassin, Étienne Balibar, and Alain de Libera, "Subject," in Cassin, *Dictionary of Untranslatables*, 1075.

39. Ezra Pound, "Cavalcanti," in *The Literary Essays of Ezra Pound*, ed. T. S. Eliot (New York: New Directions, 1954), 196.

40. Sandra Laugier, "To Translate," in Cassin, *Dictionary of Untranslatables*, 1148.

41. Stuart MacClintock, *Perversity and Error: Studies on the "Averroist" John of Jandun* (Bloomington: Indiana University Press, 1956). MacClintock's title refers not to Jean's work, it must be noted, but to

his modern commentators. See also Edward P. Mahoney, "John of Jandun," in *Routledge Encyclopedia of Philosophy*, ed. Edward Craig (London: Routledge, 1998), 5:106–8, and James B. South, "John of Jandun," in *A Companion to Philosophy in the Middle Ages*, ed. Jorge J. E. Gracia and Timothy B. Noone (Malden MA: Blackwell, 2002), 372–76.

42. Anthony Vidler, "Chôra" in Cassin, *Dictionary of Untranslatables*, 132.

43. Vidler, "Chôra," 133.

44. Vidler, "Chôra," 134.

45. Ben Kafka, "Media/Medium (of Communication)," in Cassin, *Dictionary of Untranslatables*, 626.

46. Kafka, "Media/Medium (of Communication)," 626.

47. Baldassare Castiglione, *The Book of the Courtier*, trans. Sir Thomas Hoby, ed. Walter Raleigh (London: David Nutt, 1900), 59.

48. Seamus Perry, ed., *Coleridge's Notebooks: A Selection* (Oxford: Oxford University Press, 2004), 75.

49. Emily Apter, "Preface," in Cassin, *Dictionary of Untranslatables*, xi.

50. Michael Wood, "13 Untranslatable Words," *Publishers Weekly*, April 11, 2014, http://www.publishersweekly.com/pw/by-topic/industry-news/tip-sheet/article/61813-13-untranslatable-words.html; Wood, "What 'Justice' Means around the World," *The Huffington Post*, April 17, 2014, http://www.huffingtonpost.com/michael-wood/justice-meaning_b_5161369.html; and Wood, "Translating Rilke," *World Literature Today* 88, nos. 3–4 (May–August 2014): 46.

51. See Chad Post, "Translation Database," *Three Percent* (blog), April 9, 2018, http://www.rochester.edu/College/translation/threepercent/index.php?s=database. The database is maintained and updated by *Publishers Weekly*, where it is reported that 2017 saw the publication of roughly 732 new translations, including fiction, poetry, nonfiction, and children's literature: https://www.publishersweekly.com/pw/translation/search/index.html.

52. Wood, "Translating Rilke," 46.

53. For a bibliography of translations up to 1997, see Ian Hilton, "Rainer Maria Rilke, 1875–1926," in *Encyclopedia of Literary Translation into English*, ed. Olive Classe (London: Fitzroy Dearborn, 2000), 2:1160–67.

54. Wood, "Translating Rilke," 46.

55. Wood, "Translating Rilke," 47.

56. Wood, "Translating Rilke," 47.

57. Rilke's letter, translated by Robert Vilain, is quoted by Thomas Martinec, "*The Sonnets to Orpheus*," in *The Cambridge Companion to Rilke*, ed. Karen Leeder and Robert Vilain (Cambridge: Cambridge University Press, 2010), 97. For the belated romanticism of twentieth-century Anglophone poetries, see, for example, Antony Easthope, *Englishness and National Culture* (London: Routledge, 1999), chap. 8, and Charles Altieri, *Self and Sensibility in Contemporary American Poetry* (Cambridge: Cambridge University Press, 1984), chap. 1. A more direct connection is argued in Russell T. Fowler, "Charting the 'Lost World': Rilke's Influence on Randall Jarrell," *Twentieth Century Literature* 30, no. 1 (1984): 100–122.

58. Wood, "Translating Rilke," 47, 48, 49.

59. Wood, "Translating Rilke," 48, 51.

60. Apter, *Against World Literature*, 138.

61. Apter, *Against World Literature*, 146.

62. Apter, *Against World Literature*, 145, 148.

63. Apter, *Against World Literature*, 235.

64. Apter, *Against World Literature*, 249.

65. Apter, *Against World Literature*, 284.

66. Raymond Williams, *Keywords: A Vocabulary of Culture and Society* (Oxford: Oxford University Press, 1976), 280.

67. Apter, *Against World Literature*, 296.

68. Rachel Holmes, *Eleanor Marx: A Life* (London: Bloomsbury, 2014), 253.

69. Garnett's fee is cited by Margaret Lesser, "Professionals," in *The Oxford History of Literary Translation in English, Volume 4, 1790–1900*, ed. Peter France and Kenneth Haynes (Oxford: Oxford University Press, 2006), 88. The rent figures come from the anonymous article, "Ladies' Residential Chambers," *Englishwoman's Review of Social and Industrial Questions* 20, no. 193 (1889): 271–73.

70. Apter, *Against World Literature*, 319.

71. Eleanor Marx Aveling, introduction to Gustave Flaubert, *Madame Bovary: Provincial Manners*, trans. Eleanor Marx Aveling (London: Henry Vizetelly, 1886), xxii.

72. Apter, *Against World Literature*, 247.

73. Apter, *Against World Literature*, 3.

74. Jacques Derrida, *The Monolingualism of the Other; or, The Prosthesis of Origin*, trans. Patrick Mensah (Stanford CA: Stanford University Press, 1998), 56–57.

75. Samuel Weber, *Benjamin's -abilities* (Cambridge MA: Harvard University Press, 2008), 6.

76. Apter, *Against World Literature*, 138.

77. Weber, *Benjamin's -abilities*, 91–92.

78. For the first reading, see George Steiner, *After Babel: Aspects of Language and Translation* (Oxford: Oxford University Press, 1979), 308; for the second, Jacques Derrida, "Des Tours de Babel," trans. Joseph F. Graham in *Difference in Translation*, ed. Joseph F. Graham (Ithaca NY: Cornell University Press, 1985), 201. The only commentator to have noted the possibility of both readings seems to be John Johnston, "Translation as Simulacrum," in *Rethinking Translation: Discourse, Subjectivity, Ideology*, ed. Lawrence Venuti (London: Routledge, 1992), 45–46.

79. Weber, *Benjamin's -abilities*, 59.

80. Weber, *Benjamin's -abilities*, 93.

81. Weber, *Benjamin's -abilities*, 116.

82. Jacques Derrida, "Signature Event Context," in *Margins of Philosophy*, trans. Alan Bass (Chicago: University of Chicago Press, 1982), 320.

83. Derrida, "Signature Event Context," 320.

84. Weber, *Benjamin's -abilities*, 65–66. The italicized abbreviations within brackets and parentheses refer to Walter Benjamin, *Gesammelte Schriften IV*, ed. Tillman Rexroth (Frankfurt: Suhrkamp, 1972), and *Selected Writings, Volume 1: 1913–1926*, ed. Marcus Bullock and Michael W. Jennings (Cambridge MA: Harvard University Press, 2004), which contains Harry Zohn's translation of "The Task of the Translator."

85. Carlo Salzani, "Review of Samuel Weber, *Benjamin's —abilities*," *Bryn Mawr Review of Comparative Literature* 7, no. 1 (Fall 2008), https://repository.brynmawr.edu/bmrcl/vol7/iss1/1. For an account of Harry Zohn's life and career, see Pam Saur, "In Memoriam: Harry Zohn (Nov. 21, 1932–June 3, 2001)," *Modern Austrian Literature* 34, nos. 1–2 (2001): 125–28.

86. Apter, *Against World Literature*, 99–100.

87. Robert Barsky, *Constructing a Productive Other: Discourse Theory and the Convention Refugee Hearing* (Amsterdam: Benjamins, 1994); Moira Inghilleri, *Interpreting Justice: Ethics, Politics, and Language* (Abingdon UK: Routledge, 2012); Vicente L. Rafael, "Translation in Wartime," *Public Culture* 19, no. 2 (2007): 239–46; Rafael, "Translation, American English, and the National Insecurities of Empire," *Social Text 101* 27, no. 4 (Winter 2009): 1–23.

88. Rafael, "Translation, American English, and the National Insecurities of Empire," 16, 17.

89. Rafael, "Translation, American English, and the National Insecurities of Empire," 18.

90. Rafael, "Translation, American English, and the National Insecurities of Empire," 17.

91. I discuss translation as a cultural means of resistance against multinational capitalism in *Translation Changes Everything: Theory and Practice* (Abingdon UK: Routledge, 2013), chap. 8.

92. Stéphane Hessel, *Time for Outrage: Indignez-vous!*, trans. Marion Duvert (New York: Twelve, 2011); the Invisible Committee, *The Coming Insurrection* (Los Angeles: Semiotext(e), 2009). No translator is credited.

93. Stéphane Hessel, *¡Indignaos!*, trans. Telmo Moreno Lanaspa (Madrid: Destino, 2011).

94. Matthew Harrington, "Translating Revolutionary Politics in the Nineteenth Century" (PhD diss. prospectus, Temple University, 2017), 3–4.

95. Mari C. Jones, Mair Parry, and Lynn Williams, "Sociolinguistic Variation," in *The Oxford Guide to Romance Languages*, ed. Adam Ledgeway and Martin Maiden (Oxford: Oxford University Press, 2016), 619, 622.

96. Harrington, "Translating Revolutionary Politics in the Nineteenth Century," 4.

97. Jóse Luis Sampedro, "Prólogo: Yo tambien," in Hessel, *¡Indignaos!*, 5.

2. PROVERBS OF UNTRANSLATABILITY

1. Jerome, *Liber de optimo genere interpretandi (Epistula 57)*, ed. G. J. M. Bartelink (Lugundi Batavorum: Brill, 1980), 5:2.

2. Jacques Derrida, *Le monolinguisme de l'autre ou la prothèse d'origine* (Paris: Galilée, 1996), 103; Derrida, *The Monolingualism of the Other;*

or, *The Prosthesis of Origin*, trans. Patrick Mensah (Stanford CA: Stanford University Press, 1998), 56–57.

3. George Steiner, *After Babel: Aspects of Language and Translation* (Oxford: Oxford University Press, 1979), 248, 251.

4. Jacques Derrida, "The *Retrait* of Metaphor," trans. Peggy Kamuf, in *Psyche: Inventions of the Other, Volume 1*, ed. and trans. Peggy Kamuf and Elizabeth Rottenberg (Stanford CA: Stanford University Press, 2007), 48–80.

5. I am relying on the entry, "trait," in Maria-Daniella Dick and Julian Wolfreys, *The Derrida Wordbook* (Edinburgh: Edinburgh University Press, 2013), 287.

6. Derrida, "The *Retrait* of Metaphor," 50.

7. Derrida, "The *Retrait* of Metaphor," 77.

8. Emily Austen, "A Stitch in Time," *Texas Monthly*, June 1979, http://www.texasmonthly.com/articles/a-stitch-in-time/; Diane Clay, "A Stitch in Time: Implanted Threads Tighten Skin," *The Oklahoman*, September 20, 2005, http://newsok.com/article/2912461; Lori A. Gurien et al., "A Stitch in Time Saves Nine: Suture Technique Does Not Affect Intestinal Growth in a Young, Growing Animal Model," *Journal of Pediatric Surgery* 51, no. 5 (May 2016): 819–21; Rebecca Kirk, "Lung Cancer: Maintenance Chemotherapy—A Stitch in Time Saves Nine?," *Nature Reviews Clinical Oncology* 9, no. 4 (April 2012): 187.

9. Shareen Robin, "A Stitch in Time Saves Nine: Pre-marital Health Check-Ups a Necessity," *ClueBunch*, October 30, 2014, http://cluebunch.com/stitch-time-saves-nine-pre-marital-health-check-ups-necessity/.

10. Thomas Fuller, *Gnomologia: Adagies and Proverbs, Wise Sentences and Witty Sayings, Ancient and Modern, Foreign and British* (London: B. Barker, 1732), 283.

11. W. G. Smith, ed., *The Oxford Dictionary of English Proverbs*, rev. F. P. Wilson, 3rd ed. (Oxford: Clarendon Press, 1970), 835; Susan Ratcliffe, ed., *Oxford Treasury of Sayings and Quotations*, 4th ed. (Oxford: Oxford University Press, 2011), 465.

12. D. M. Stevenson, "Trade with South America," *The Times of London*, August 7, 1929, 3.

13. Arthur Sze, ed. and trans., *The Silk Dragon: Translations from the Chinese* (Port Townsend WA: Copper Canyon Press, 2001), 3.

14. Roman Jakobson, "On Linguistic Aspects of Translation" (1959), in *The Translation Studies Reader*, 3rd ed., ed. Lawrence Venuti (Abingdon UK: Routledge, 2012), 131.

15. Jakobson, "On Linguistic Aspects of Translation," 127.

16. Niccolò Franco, *Le pistole vulgari* (Venice: Antonio Gardane, 1539). See Paolo Cherchi, "Traduttore Traditore," *Lingua Nostra* 67, nos. 1–2 (March–June 2006): 59.

17. Franco, *Le pistole vulgari*, 85v.

18. Henri Estienne, *L'introduction au traitté de la conformité des merveilles anciennes avec les modernes: ou, traitté preparatif à l'Apologie pour Herodote. L'argument est pris de l'Apolog. pour Herodote, composée en latin par Henri Estienne, et est ici continué par luy-mesme* (Lyon: Benoist Rigaud, 1592), B6r–B6v.

19. Henri Estienne, *A World of Wonders: or, An Introduction to a Treatise Touching the Conformitie of Ancient and Moderne Wonders: or, A Preparative Treatise to the Apologie for Herodotus. The Argument whereof is taken from the Apologie for Herodotus, written in Latine by Henry Stephen, and continued here by the Author himselfe*, trans. Richard Carew (Edinburgh: Andrew Hart and Richard Lawson, 1608), cv.

20. Jean Nicot, *Thresor de la langue françoyse, tant ancienne que moderne* (Paris: David Douceur, 1606); Randle Cotgrave, *A Dictionarie of the French and English Tongues* (London: Adam Islip, 1611).

21. Estienne, *A World of Wonders*, A4r.

22. Estienne, *A World of Wonders*, A4r.

23. A. E. B. Coldiron, "Commonplaces and Metaphors," in *The Oxford History of Literary Translation in English, Volume 2, 1550–1660*, ed. Gordon Braden, Robert Cummings, and Stuart Gillespie (Oxford: Oxford University Press, 2011), 112.

24. Estienne, *A World of Wonders*, A4r.

25. Sir William Cornwallis, *Essayes* (London: Edmund Mattes, 1600), c3v–D4r.

26. Estienne, *A World of Wonders*, A4r.

27. John H. Astington, *Actors and Acting in Shakespeare's Time: The Art of Stage Playing* (Cambridge: Cambridge University Press, 2010), 37.

28. Joachim Du Bellay, *The Regrets with The Antiquities of Rome, Three Latin Elegies, and The Defense and Enrichment of the French Language*,

ed. and trans. Richard Helgerson (Philadelphia: University of Pennsylvania Press, 2006), 335, 337, 336.

29. Charlton T. Lewis and Charles Short, *A Latin Dictionary* (Oxford: Clarendon Press, 1879), s.v. "genius"; Alain Pons, "Genius," trans. Nathaneal Stein, in *Dictionary of Untranslatables: A Philosophical Lexicon*, ed. Barbara Cassin, trans. Steven Rendall et al., translation edited by Emily Apter, Jacques Lezra, and Michael Wood (Princeton NJ: Princeton University Press, 2014), 380.

30. Nicot, *Thresor de la langue françoyse*, s.v. "genre," where the word is defined as "genus humanum."

31. Du Bellay, *The Regrets*, 337, 336.

32. Du Bellay, *The Regrets*, 335, 334.

33. Lewis and Short, *A Latin Dictionary*, s.v. "gigno."

34. Margaret B. Wells, "What Did du Bellay Understand by Translation?," *Forum for Modern Language Studies* 16, no. 2 (1980): 175–85.

35. Du Bellay, *The Regrets*, 347, 346.

36. Du Bellay, *The Regrets*, 335, 334.

37. Du Bellay, *The Regrets*, 347, 346.

38. Du Bellay, *The Regrets*, 347, 346.

39. Giuseppe Giusti, *Proverbi toscani*, ed. Gino Capponi (Florence: A spese dell'editore, 1873), 179; Robert Christy, *Proverbs, Maxims and Phrases of All Ages, Classified Subjectively and Arranged Alphabetically* (New York: G. P. Putnam's Sons, 1888), 2:372.

40. Richard Chenevix Trench, *On the Lessons in Proverbs: Five Lectures. Being the Substance of Lectures Delivered to Young Men's Societies at Portsmouth and Elsewhere* (London: John W. Parker, 1853), 28–29.

41. Antoine Berman, "Translation and the Trials of the Foreign" (1985), trans. Lawrence Venuti, in Venuti, *The Translation Studies Reader*, 252. See also Berman, "L'essence platonicienne de la traduction," *Revue d'Esthetique* 12 (1986): 63–73.

42. John Frederick Nims, "Traduttore Traditore: Campbell's St. John of the Cross," *Poetry* 80, no. 3 (June 1952): 153.

43. Nims, "Traduttore Traditore," 153, 158.

44. Christopher Reid, "A Match for Macchu Picchu," *London Review of Books*, June 4, 1981, 16.

45. David Damrosch, *What Is World Literature?* (Princeton NJ: Princeton University Press, 2003), 288.

46. Damrosch, *What Is World Literature?*, 289.

47. Louis Untermeyer, *Robert Frost: A Backward Look* (Washington DC: Library of Congress, 1964), 18.

48. Cleanth Brooks and Robert Penn Warren, eds., *Conversations on the Craft of Poetry* (New York: Holt, Rinehart and Winston, 1961), 7.

49. Samuel Taylor Coleridge, *Specimens of the Table Talk of the Late Samuel Taylor Coleridge*, ed. Henry Nelson Coleridge (New York: Harper and Brothers, 1835), 76.

50. *The Letters of Robert Frost, Volume 1: 1886–1920*, ed. Donald Sheehy, Mark Richardson, and Robert Faggen (Cambridge MA: Harvard University Press, 2014), 122, 173, 174.

51. *The Letters of Robert Frost*, 123.

52. *The Letters of Robert Frost*, 248.

53. *The Letters of Robert Frost*, 173.

54. *The Letters of Robert Frost*, 234.

55. William Stanley Braithwaite, "Robert Frost, New American Poet," *Boston Evening Transcript*, May 8, 1915, part three, 10.

56. Thom Satterlee, "Robert Frost's Views on Translation," *Delos* 9 (1996): 49.

57. Untermeyer, *Robert Frost*, 18.

58. *The Letters of Robert Frost*, 234.

59. *The Odyssey of Homer; Books I–XII*, trans. George Herbert Palmer (Boston: Houghton Mifflin, 1884), xi.

60. *The Collected Prose of Robert Frost*, ed. Mark Richardson (Cambridge MA: Harvard University Press, 2007), 123. The full title of Weeks's book is *Books We Like; Sixty-Two Answers to the Question: "Please choose, and give reasons for your choice, ten books, exclusive of the Bible and Shakespeare, dictionaries, encyclopedias, and other ordinary reference books, that you believe should be in every public library"* (Boston: Massachusetts Library Association, 1936).

61. *The Odyssey of Homer, Translated into English Prose*, trans. T. E. Shaw (New York: Oxford University Press, 1932), n.p.

62. *The Odyssey of Homer*, trans. Palmer, v.

63. *The Odyssey of Homer*, trans. Palmer, v.

64. *The Odyssey of Homer*, trans. Palmer, v–vi.

65. *The Odyssey of Homer*, trans. Palmer, vi–vii.

66. *The Odyssey of Homer*, trans. Palmer, viii.

67. *The Odyssey of Homer*, trans. Palmer, vi–vii.

68. Emily Apter, *The Translation Zone: A New Comparative Literature* (Princeton NJ: Princeton University Press, 2006), 85, 226.

69. Derrida, *Le monolingualisme de l'autre*, 102; Derrida, *The Monolingualism of the Other*, 56.

70. Jacques Derrida, "What Is a 'Relevant' Translation?," trans. Lawrence Venuti, *Critical Inquiry* 27, no. 2 (2001): 179.

71. Derrida, "What Is a 'Relevant' Translation?," 181.

72. Derrida, *The Monolingualism of the Other*, 56.

73. Derrida, "What Is a 'Relevant' Translation?," 179; Derrida, "Qu'est-ce qu'une traduction 'relevante'?" in *Quinzièmes assises de la traduction littéraire (Arles 1998)* (Arles: Actes Sud, 1999), 26.

74. Jacques Derrida, "Différance," in *Margins of Philosophy*, trans. Alan Bass (Chicago: University of Chicago Press, 1982), 1–28.

75. Derrida, "What Is a 'Relevant' Translation?," 181.

76. Derrida, *The Monolingualism of the Other*, 56.

77. Derrida, "What Is a 'Relevant' Translation?," 183–94.

78. Derrida, "What Is a 'Relevant' Translation?," 194, 195.

79. Derrida, "Qu'est-ce qu'une traduction 'relevante'?," 42; Derrida, "What Is a 'Relevant' Translation?," 195.

80. Derrida, "What Is a 'Relevant' Translation?," 196.

81. Derrida, "What Is a 'Relevant' Translation?," 198.

82. Derrida, "What Is a 'Relevant' Translation?," 198.

83. Derrida, "What Is a 'Relevant' Translation?," 197.

84. Derrida, "What Is a 'Relevant' Translation?," 194.

85. Derrida, "What Is a 'Relevant' Translation?," 198, 199.

3. THE TROUBLE WITH SUBTITLES

1. For accounts of this emergence, see Javier Franco and Pilar Orero, "Research on Audiovisual Translation: Some Objective Conclusions, or The Birth of an Academic Field," in *Research on Translation for Subtitling in Spain and Italy*, ed. J. D. Sanderson (Alicante: Universidad de Alicante, 2005), 79–92, and Luis Pérez-González, *Audiovisual Translation: Theories, Methods and Issues* (Abingdon UK: Routledge, 2014), especially 26–27.

2. Jan Pedersen, *Subtitling Norms for Television: An Exploration Focusing on Extralinguistic Cultural Factors* (Amsterdam: Benjamins, 2011), 11.

3. Christine Sponholz, "Teaching Audiovisual Translation: Theoretical Aspects, Market Requirements, University Training and Curriculum Development," Diplomarbeit, Fachbereich Angewandte Sprach- und Kulturwissenschaft, Johannes Gutenberg-Universität Mainz, 2003, 16, 59, http://sign-dialog.de/wp-content/diplomarbeit _200211_sponholz_teachingaudiovisualtranslation.pdf.

4. Henrik Gottlieb, "Subtitling—A New University Discipline," in *Teaching Translation and Interpreting*, ed. Cay Dollerup and A. Loddegaard (Amsterdam: Benjamins, 1992), 164–65.

5. Henrik Gottlieb, "Subtitling," in *Routledge Encyclopedia of Translation Studies*, ed. Mona Baker with Kirsten Malmkjær (London: Routledge, 1998), 247.

6. Gottlieb, "Subtitling," 247.

7. Gottlieb, "Subtitling," 247.

8. Pedersen, *Subtitling Norms for Television*, 21. Here Pedersen is referring to Henrik Gottlieb, *Subtitles, Translation and Idioms* (Copenhagen: Center for Translation Studies, University of Copenhagen, 1997), 101.

9. Gottlieb, "Subtitling," 247.

10. Jorge Díaz-Cintas and Aline Remael, *Audiovisual Translation: Subtitling* (Manchester UK: St. Jerome Publishing, 2007; Abingdon UK: Routledge, 2014), 148.

11. *Psycho*, directed by Alfred Hitchcock (Shamley Productions/Paramount Pictures, 1960).

12. The subtitles are cited in Panayota Georgakopoulou, "Subtitling for the DVD Industry," in *Audiovisual Translation: Language Transfer on Screen*, ed. Jorge Díaz-Cintas and Gunilla Anderman (Basingstoke UK: Palgrave Macmillan, 2009), 24.

13. Georgakopoulou, "Subtitling for the DVD Industry," 23.

14. Díaz-Cintas and Remael, *Audiovisual Translation*, 185.

15. Pedersen, *Subtitling Norms for Television*, 43.

16. Quoted in Pedersen, *Subtitling Norms for Television*, 91, from Joan Darling, dir., "The Nurses," written by Linda Bloodworth, *M*A*S*H*, season 5, episode 6, October 19, 1976.

17. Pedersen, *Subtitling Norms for Television*, 91. The English back translation is Pedersen's.

18. Pedersen, *Subtitling Norms for Television*, 92.

19. Eugene Nida, *Towards a Science of Translating, with Special Reference to Principles and Procedures Involved in Bible Translating* (Leiden: Brill, 1964), 159.

20. See Ted Okuda with Edward Watz, *The Columbia Shorts: Two-Reel Hollywood Film Comedies* (Jefferson NC: McFarland, 1986), 60, and James Niebaur, "The Stooges, At Last, Get Some Respect," *Cineaste* 29, no. 1 (2003): 12.

21. Pedersen, *Subtitling Norms for Television*, 91.

22. Henri Béhar, "Cultural Ventriloquism," in *Subtitles: On the Foreignness of Film*, ed. Atom Egoyan and Ian Balfour (Cambridge MA: MIT Press, 2004), 85; *Thérèse*, directed by Alain Cavalier (AFC/Centre National de la Cinématographie/Films A2, 1986).

23. Béhar, "Cultural Ventriloquism," 82.

24. Pérez-González, *Audiovisual Translation*, 34, 49–54.

25. Subtitling conventions are discussed by Díaz-Cintas and Remael, *Audiovisual Translation*, chaps. 6 and 7.

26. Pérez-González, *Audiovisual Translation*, 53, which includes the emphasis.

27. I discuss this discursive regime and its consequences for translators and the practice of translation in *The Translator's Invisibility: A History of Translation*, 2nd ed. (Abingdon UK: Routledge, 2008), chap. 1.

28. Interview with Henri Béhar, April 8, 2017. Both Béhar and Pollack are credited on the 35 mm print at the Harvard Film Archive, the VHS released by the Circle Releasing Corp. in 1986, and the DVD released by Wellspring Media in 2002. My efforts to locate Pollack for an interview have been unsuccessful.

29. Béhar, "Cultural Ventriloquism," 85.

30. *Annie Hall*, directed by Woody Allen (Rollins-Joffe Productions/ United Artists, 1977). The screenplay is quoted from Woody Allen and Marshall Brickman, *Annie Hall* (London: Faber and Faber, 2000), 9–10.

31. *Annie Hall*, directed by Woody Allen (MGM Home Entertainment, 1998, DVD). In the discussion that follows, I cite the French and Spanish subtitles from this DVD.

32. Woody Allen and Marshall Brickman, *Annie Hall*, trans. José Luis Guarner (Barcelona: Tusquets, 1999), 20–21.

33. Paul Ricoeur, *Freud and Philosophy: An Essay in Interpretation*, trans. Denis Savage (New Haven CT: Yale University Press, 1970), chap. 1. I provide further examples of the critical dialectic between translations and their source texts in *Translation Changes Everything: Theory and Practice* (Abingdon UK: Routledge, 2013), chaps. 4, 10, 11, 13.

34. Christopher Taylor, "Pedagogical Tools for Training Subtitlers," in Díaz-Cintas and Anderman, *Audiovisual Translation*, 218, 225, 226.

35. Taylor, "Pedagogical Tools for Training Subtitlers," 218.

36. Taylor, "Pedagogical Tools for Training Subtitlers," 218, 219.

37. Taylor, "Pedagogical Tools for Training Subtitlers," 217–18, 225.

38. *Du rififi chez les hommes*, directed by Jules Dassin (Pathé-Consortium Cinéma, 1955). Quotations of subtitles are drawn from *Rififi*, directed by Jules Dassin (New York Film Annex, 1998, VHS) and *Rififi* (Criterion Collection, 2001, DVD).

39. Bosley Crowther, "Screen: Tough Paris Crime Story; 'Rififi,' About a Jewel Theft, at Fine Arts," *New York Times*, June 6, 1956, 37.

40. Author interview with Lenny Borger, February 5, 2017.

41. J. Hoberman, "Bands of Outsiders," *Village Voice*, July 25, 2000, 119.

42. *The Asphalt Jungle*, directed by John Huston (Metro-Goldwyn-Mayer, 1950).

43. Dudley Andrew, "An Atlas of World Cinema," in *Remapping World Cinema: Identity, Culture and Politics in Film*, ed. Stephanie Dennison and Song Hwee-Lin (London: Wallflower Press, 2006), 23.

44. Alastair Phillips, *Rififi* (London: I. B. Tauris, 2009), 76, 75.

45. Abé Mark Nornes, *Cinema Babel: Translating Global Cinema* (Minneapolis: University of Minnesota Press, 2007), 159, 156, 176–77.

46. Nornes, *Cinema Babel*, 155, 179; Pérez-González, *Audiovisual Translation*, 52.

47. Nornes, *Cinema Babel*, 185.

48. Nornes, *Cinema Babel*, 179.

49. Nornes, *Cinema Babel*, 180.

50. Nornes, *Cinema Babel*, 187.

51. Nornes, *Cinema Babel*, 182–84; Pérez-González, *Audiovisual Translation*, 78–82.

52. Pérez-González, *Audiovisual Translation*, 256, 80.

53. *Thirst*, directed by Park Chan-wook (CJ Entertainment/Moho Films/ Focus Features International, 2009). The DVD version was released by Universal Studios Home Entertainment in 2009.

54. Esther Kwon's website documents her work: http://www.remeta.net/.

55. Author interview with Wonjo Jeong, February 16, 2017.

56. Key documents in the debates provoked by auteur theory are gathered in John Caughie, ed., *Theories of Authorship*, rev. ed. (Abingdon UK: Routledge, 2013).

57. Alan C. L. Yu takes a linguistics-oriented approach in *A Natural History of Infixation* (Oxford: Oxford University Press, 2007).

58. Stan Carey, "Absoposilutely Infixed," *Sentence First* (blog), October 7, 2011, https://stancarey.wordpress.com/2011/10/07/absoposilutely -infixed/.

59. Author interview with Esther Kwon, February 7, 2017.

60. *The Exorcist*, directed by William Friedkin (Hoya Productions, 1973).

61. Robert L. Cagle, "The Good, the Bad, and the South Korean: Violence, Morality, and the South Korean Extreme Film," in *Horror to the Extreme: Changing Boundaries in Asian Cinema*, ed. Jinhee Choi and Mitsuyo Wada-Marciano (Hong Kong: Hong Kong University Press, 2009), 125.

62. Pérez-González, *Audiovisual Translation*, 187.

63. Christopher Taylor, "Multimodal Transcription in the Analysis, Translation and Subtitling of Italian Films," *The Translator* 9, no. 2 (2003): 195.

STOP/START

1. Gilles Deleuze and Félix Guattari, *Anti-Oedipus: Capitalism and Schizophrenia*, trans. Robert Hurley, Mark Seem, and Helen R. Lane (Minneapolis: University of Minnesota Press, 1983), 36.

2. Catherine Belsey, *Critical Practice* (London: Methuen, 1980), 91. See also Steve Neale, "Propaganda," *Screen*, 18, no. 3 (1977): 31.

3. See Andrew Benjamin, *Translation and the Nature of Philosophy: A New Theory of Words* (London: Routledge, 1989), chap. 1.

4. For an approach to reading translations as texts in their own right, see Lawrence Venuti, *Translation Changes Everything: Theory and Practice* (Abingdon UK: Routledge, 2013), 109–15.

To order or obtain more information on these or other University of
Nebraska Press titles, visit nebraskapress.unl.edu.

CPSIA information can be obtained
at www.ICGtesting.com
Printed in the USA
LVHW041826241019
635245LV00004B/337/P

9 781496 205131